GEORGE WASHINGTON
FRONTIER COLONEL

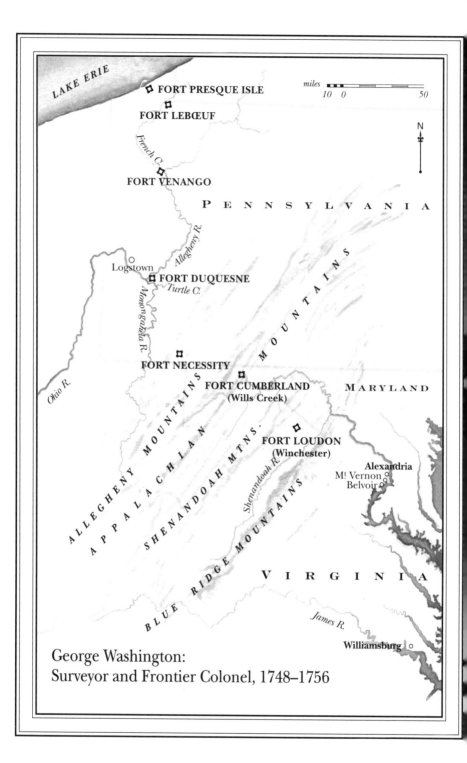

FORT PRESQUE ISLE

LAKE ERIE

FORT LEBŒUF

French C.

FORT VENANGO

P E N N S Y L V A N I A

Allegheny R.

Logstown

FORT DUQUESNE

Turtle C.

Monongahela R.

M O U N T A I N S

FORT NECESSITY

FORT CUMBERLAND
(Wills Creek)

M A R Y L A N D

Ohio R.

A L L E G H E N Y   M O U N T A I N S

A P P A L A C H I A N

S H E N A N D O A H   M T N S.

FORT LOUDON
(Winchester)

Shenandoah R.

Alexandria
M! Vernon
Belvoir

B L U E   R I D G E   M O U N T A I N S

V I R G I N I A

James R.

Williamsburg

miles
10   0   50

N

George Washington:
Surveyor and Frontier Colonel, 1748–1756

MARYLAND

FUTURE SITE OF
WASHINGTON D.C.

Annapolis

Alexandria

Mount Vernon
Belvoir

N

miles

0   30

Ferry Farm
Fredericksburg

Pope's Cr.

VIRGINIA

Potomac R.

CHESAPEAKE BAY

Rappahannock R.

Richmond

York R.

Williamsburg
Yorktown

James R.

George Washington's Virginia

Norfolk

GEORGE WASHINGTON FRONTIER COLONEL

STERLING NORTH

STERLING PUBLISHING CO., INC.
New York

A FLYING POINT PRESS BOOK

Design: PlutoMedia
Front cover painting: "A Charming Field for an Encounter" by Robert Griffing,
courtesy of Paramount Press [Editor's note: This historically accurate
painting depicts George Washington and his troops
outside Fort Necessity just before battle.]

Library of Congress Cataloging-in-Publication Data Available

2 4 6 8 10 9 7 5 3 1

Published by Sterling Publishing Co., Inc.
387 Park Avenue South, New York, NY 10016
Original edition published by Random House, Inc.
Copyright © 1957 by Gladys North
New material in this updated edition
Copyright © 2006 by Flying Point Press
Maps copyright © by Richard Thompson, Creative Freelancers, Inc.
Distributed in Canada by Sterling Publishing
c/o Canadian Manda Group, 165 Dufferin Street
Toronto, Ontario, Canada M6K 3H6
Distributed in the United Kingdom by GMC Distribution Services
Castle Place, 166 High Street, Lewes, East Sussex, England BN7 1XU
Distributed in Australia by Capricorn Link (Australia) Pty. Ltd.
P.O. Box 704, Windsor, NSW 2756, Australia

Sterling ISBN-13: 978-1-4027-3611-7
ISBN-10: 1-4027-3611-8

For information about custom editions, special sales, premium and
corporate purchases, please contact Sterling Special Sales
Department at 800-805-5489 or specialsales@sterlingpub.com.

For my son, David

CONTENTS

GEORGE WASHINGTON
FRONTIER COLONEL

A BABY CHRISTENED GEORGE

"THE WIND IN THE NIGHT INCREASED TO A MERE STORM and raind exceed'g hard; towards day it moderated and ceased Raining but the whole day afterwards was Squally." Thus George Washington, in his copper-plate handwriting, reported the weather of February 22, 1760—exactly twenty-eight years after his birth.

Perhaps it was just such a typical February day in 1732 when "about 10 in The Morning" (to quote the family Bible) a lusty boy named George was born to Mary Ball Washington and her husband Augustine. Their modest plantation house stood on a low bluff above the widening

3

waters of Pope's Creek where it enters the Potomac River in Tidewater, Virginia.

The twenty-four-year-old mother has been described as a handsome woman of medium height, with a well-rounded figure and a pleasing voice. She has also been described as luxury-loving and slightly spoiled. She had acquired by inheritance some land, a few slaves, several riding horses and a "good silk plush riding saddle." She loved to dance, and appears to have enjoyed excellent health. Despite her "deathly fear of thunder storms" she lived beyond her 80th birthday.

Augustine Washington the father, known to his friends as "Gus," has been portrayed as a man of great strength, six feet tall, well-proportioned and blond. Although he owned vast tracts of land and a part interest in iron mines and furnaces, he was not a particularly successful businessman. Kindly by nature and fond of children, he must have been deeply moved as he looked down upon his young wife and her first child.

Perhaps the slave boy who kept the many hearths burning was now called to replenish the fire. Possibly a slave girl from the separate building that housed the kitchen now brought hot broth for the tired mother. Let the wind buffet the wide Potomac into seething crests of foam. Let the gulls go crying over the stormy water. Inside the plantation house in the fire-lit bedroom all was warm and secure.

At about this point one can visualize a little girl of nine tiptoeing into the room to have her first look at her new half-brother. Her name was Jane, and she was the youngest of three living children by a former wife of Augustine Washington, a woman no longer living. Besides this half-sister, little George had two big half-brothers attending Appleby School far across the sea in England. The eldest was a boy of fourteen named Lawrence, a brave and gentle person who would later have great influence in shaping George's character. The other half-brother, Augustine, Jr., was known to the family as "Austin." He was a year or two younger than Lawrence. These three—Lawrence, Austin and Jane—furnished a ready-made family for the first child of Mary Ball Washington.

It is undeniable that George Washington had many advantages from birth. One hundred and twenty-five years had passed since the first hopeful settlers had come to Jamestown. Never again would Virginia know a "starving time." Plantations were well established along the James, the York, the Rappahannock and the Potomac—those beautiful rivers running into the Chesapeake.

But not all of these plantations were equally large or productive. On some the fertility was already impaired by years of tobacco planting. Some owners prospered, some did not. Despite his many acres, Augustine Washington was not a really rich man by modern standards nor even by the standards of his own day. The Carters, the Fairfaxes and many other Virginia planters were far wealthier.

More important than any material wealth George would inherit was his endowment of good health, a good brain and a sound family tradition. In these he was rich indeed.

In 1732 when George Washington was born into the fourth generation of his paternal family in America, the Washingtons had been on the Potomac for seventy-five years. It was possibly in just such stormy weather that John Washington, Mate of a sailing ketch called the *Sea Horse of London*, came scudding up the windswept waters of the Potomac in the year 1657. Later the little ship went aground and was sunk. But the Mate's story has a happy ending. He married the daughter of a wealthy planter and acquired a large plantation between Mattox Creek and Pope's Creek. John's eldest son was named Lawrence. One of Lawrence's sons was Augustine—the tall, blond Gus who now stood looking down at his small son, George.

Great-grandfather John, grandfather Lawrence and father August—each of this direct male line had added land to the family holdings. Each had been a Justice of the Peace, a member of the Virginia House of Burgesses, and an officer in the Virginia Militia. And each had enjoyed at least a few years' schooling "back home" in England—a privilege George was never to be granted.

Possibly this healthy boy, soon to be christened George, could hope to be as locally important as his father, grandfather and great-grandfather. But no one that February day in 1732 could have predicted that this son of Mary and Augustine Washington would one day be called The Father of His Country— "First in war, first in peace and first in the hearts of his countrymen."

CHAPTER 2

CHILDHOOD ON
THE POTOMAC

WHEN GEORGE WASHINGTON WAS BORN THERE WERE, of course, no automobiles, airplanes, locomotives or steamboats, nor was there electricity and modern plumbing. Men, animals, wind and falling water provided most of the harnessed energy. In that year young Louis XV was on the throne of France. George II was the King of England. The most widely known American was a 26-year-old Philadelphia printer named Benjamin Franklin. It would be two more years before Daniel Boone would be born—one of the few frontiersmen who would see more action in the wilderness than George Washington himself.

At the Pope's Creek plantation, George knew nothing of such matters. He ate, slept, played with his pets and watched long-legged colts frisking in the pastures. He was warned not to fall into the shallow waters of Pope's Creek. The fenced-in kitchen garden was a safe place for him to play. Here the mockingbirds sang by day and the whippoorwills called at night. Roses grew along the grassy walks between the well-kept beds of vegetables and flowers. The herb garden of sage, thyme, rosemary, pennyroyal and rue reminded him of the good odors of things cooking in the kitchen. George found ripe strawberries hiding under green leaves. All of his life he would enjoy gardens and orchards, planting and improving his fruit trees and his flowers.

When does memory begin? Perhaps George Washington's first clear recollections were of the bustle and confusion of moving from his birthplace to another great farm which Augustine owned farther up the Potomac at Little Hunting Creek (This was a 2,500-acre plantation that would later become famous as Mount Vernon.) What noise and excitement as the slaves and workmen prepared the furniture, farm tools and livestock for this big adventure!

It is probable that a small house already stood on the present site of the white-pillared mansion when the Washingtons moved in 1735 to that imposing bluff above the "River of Swans" at the "Freshes" of the Potomac. The word "Freshes" refers to the fact that the water here is less salty than farther down the river, being constantly refreshed by the Great Falls of the Potomac some twenty-four miles upstream.

The members of the Washington family making this move were five in number: Augustine the father, Mary the mother, and their children George, Betty and Samuel, ages three, two and one. George's half-sister Jane had died within the year. His half-brothers, Lawrence and Austin, were still at school in England.

Three more children were to be born to Mary Ball Washington within the next few years: John Augustine, called "Jack," in 1736; Charles in 1738; and Mildred, in 1739—a child who did not survive infancy.

George, eldest and strongest of this tribe, quite probably led the others in their adventures. He would have been the first to learn the dangerous thrill of riding horseback on some small mount, with the wind in his ginger-colored hair and the ground speeding backward under flying hoofs.

11

Augustine would certainly have taken his children to see the mill he had built at Dogue Run for grinding flour and corn meal. One can imagine the row of youngsters standing entranced as they watched the clear water tumbling over the mossy water wheel. Inside the dusty mill, the rumble of the millstones and the groaning of the wooden cogwheels may have frightened the smaller children.

Equally exciting to the young Washingtons were the activities at the private wharf on the Potomac. Here, probably under some watchful adult eye, they could fish or lie in the sun idly viewing the barges being rowed by slaves across the water to the Maryland shore. Sails were often visible, tacking into the wind or skimming like floating leaves ahead of a stiff breeze. Wild ducks and geese wedged over, high above them.

On memorable occasions the children were chased off the wharf to watch from a safe distance the loading of huge hogsheads of leaf tobacco into a three-masted, ocean-going ship. This was the harvest of an entire season of planting being freighted off to some merchant in England. Here in its finished form was the crop they had watched all year, from the tiny green plants raised so carefully in covered beds, through the transplanting, cultivating, harvesting and stripping of the pungent leaves. What back-breaking labor had gone into the production of each of those great barrels of leaf tobacco upon which depended the success of the entire plantation!

Augustine and Mary made a long list of goods they wanted the ship's captain to bring back from England. They could grow most of their own food, but they needed from the mother country many things not made in Virginia. Fine cloth for suits and dresses, for example, was not to be had in the new land. Handkerchiefs, too, and bright ribbons, warm gloves and shoes of leather were obtainable only from abroad. Nor was that all. By British restriction, farming tools such as sickles, hoes, axes and saws could not be fashioned in the colonies, so these too must come from England. And, of course, green tea and Cheshire cheese; yes, even a few toys and sweets for the children if the tobacco fetched a good price that year. What a day it must have been when the ship returned loaded with at least some of these treasures (even if the shoes were not a perfect fit and a few of the items had been ruined by sea water)!

It was from this wharf that Augustine had sailed away on another worried business trip to England. He was to attend a conference concerning those troublesome iron mines and furnaces which were earning almost nothing for himself or for his English partners. Mary and her children must have watched the sails of that departing ship until they disappeared far down the Potomac on the way to the angry Atlantic Ocean. Months later the head of the family was safely home again with news that Lawrence would soon be following. Already this big brother was something of a hero in the mind of six-year-old George.

But the happiness the Washingtons had known at Little Hunting creek was suddenly threatened by the news that Augustine had again made the decision to move, this time to a little farm on the narrow Rappahannock. They would leave behind them the beautiful "River of Swans," the wide green meadows, the cool deep forests and the plantation house on the bluff—a place which from his childhood to the day of his death George Washington so greatly loved.

CHAPTER 3

THE YEARS AT
FERRY FARM

THE NEW FARM TO WHICH THE WASHINGTONS MOVED
late in 1738 had an eight-room house situated pleasantly
on high land overlooking the river. On the far shore lay the
village of Fredericksburg. Some two miles up river, the
Falls of the Rappahannock marked the head of navigation.
Below the falls the water was deep enough for ocean-
going vessels.

There were few waking moments in which a boy could
have been unaware of this ribbon of water lying to the west
of the house—a place to swim and fish, and a highway for
the ships serving the tobacco port of Fredericksburg.

Tying the farm more closely to the river was the ferry which gave the name "Ferry Farm" to this new home of the Washingtons. The road to the Ferry ran down a steep ravine so near the house that the shouting of the teamsters and the rumble of the heavy carts may have disturbed Mary. However, to George and the other children, the ferryboat playing back and forth across the river must have seemed continuously exciting.

Equally interesting was the little town of Fredericksburg lying in neat squares on the far side of the Rappahannock. Here were tobacco warehouses; wharves; a stone quarry; and a scattering of houses. The town boasted a church, a prison, a tavern, and soon an apothecary shop where medicines were sold. Twice yearly to this village came the joyous and rowdy fairs.

Very little is known about Washington's early years. Several writers have invented unlikely stories. No one now believes that George cut down a cherry tree and then hurried to his father to confess, "I can't tell a lie, Pa, you know I can't tell a lie. I did cut it with my hatchet." This fable and many others were created from thin air by Parson M. L. Weems, a sentimental early biographer.

Equally doubtful are many of the stories about Washington's schooling. Was he instructed by a gravedigger named Hobby? There is no written evidence to prove it.

Possibly he went to a little school in Fredericksburg run by a Reverend James Marye. But if at this school he was a leader in the vigorous sports of the schoolyard, the Parson Weems must be in error when he pictures George as stopping every squabble between other boys, or rushing "instantly" to the school master to ". . . inform him of their barbarous intentions."

Somehow, between his seventh and eleventh years, he learned "reading, writing and ciphering" and a few words of Latin. He had at least one lesson in music. Obviously he mastered the art of copying his assignments in a clear, firm hand. Little more can be stated with assurance.

In view of the family tradition, it seems mysterious that George was not sent "back home" to England for a few years of study. Perhaps his father's financial troubles prevented it. Or possibly his mother wished to keep her eldest son beside her, fearing to let him cross the wind-swept North Atlantic. We do know that very soon she would be refusing to let him become a sailor.

• • •

His two half-brothers had now returned to Virginia. It was during those years that George became well acquainted with Lawrence, an admirable young man in his early twenties. George, like many boys of his age, needed a hero to worship. He saw in this intelligent and affectionate half-brother a picture of the 18th century Virginia gentleman at his best.

Doubtless Lawrence became an even greater idol in the boy's eyes when he donned the handsome uniform of a Virginia officer and shipped off with his regiment. He was serving under Admiral Vernon who had been ordered to capture the rich Spanish colonial city of Cartagena in the Caribbean. The Admiral was a brave fleet commander with important victories to his credit. But at Cartagena fortune frowned. An epidemic of yellow fever staggered the English and Virginians, helping the Spaniards to beat off the attack.

Lawrence managed to survive the campaign and to make his way back to Virginia, but he never again completely regained his health. He remodeled and enlarged the "mansion house" at Little Hunting Creek and renamed the estate "Mount Vernon" in honor of the Admiral under whom he had served. Now George had additional reasons for visiting the beloved plantation where he could listen to Lawrence tell of the recent bloody struggle with the Spanish—mortal enemies of the English since the days of Drake and the Spanish Armada.

George was not at Mount Vernon, but was visiting other relatives in Chotank in the Easter season of 1743 when a messenger came riding with the grim news that his father lay dying. George, who at eleven was already an excellent horseman, raced homeward and arrived in time to speak to his father before he died. Now Mary was alone in the world with their five surviving children, the oldest being George. Despite the provisions of the will, life would never thereafter seem completely secure to the mother of George Washington.

Augustine followed the custom of the time in leaving to his oldest son the largest portion: Lawrence was willed Mount Vernon. Austin received the Pope's Creek place. George was bequeathed Ferry Farm. And all of the other boys were left farms. Betty was to have £400. Slaves and personal property were divided among the survivors. The widow, in addition to slaves and one fifth of the personal property, would have the crops from several plantations for a number of years and the use of the farms belonging to her own sons until they came of age.

It is important to establish the fact that George at the age of eleven had not suddenly become a rich landowner. He would be twenty-one before he came into actual possession of his rather small and infertile farm. Unless he swiftly demonstrated ability as a businessmen and a willingness to work and save his money, he might easily slip back into the semi-poverty of the smaller farmers who made no more than a meager living from the Virginia soil.

The widow, despite the provisions of the will, had some reason to worry. She was not an exceptionally good manager. She had five small children and great responsibilities. More than ever she must have turned her hopes toward her oldest son.

It is difficult today to understand why there was no greater warmth between these two. It seems evident that Mary Washington was in some ways a difficult woman— proud, rather selfish, and not always just. In later years she sometimes embarrassed her famous son by claiming to be poverty-stricken, which was not the truth! George was always correct, dutiful and financially generous toward his mother. But he too had pride and a will of his own. A modern reader may sometimes wonder if too great emphasis was not placed upon mere manners in the 18th century. Polished and correct conduct is never enough. Duty and honor need to be deepened and enriched by a more important virtue—unselfish love.

George Washington must have given his mother hapiness as he copied in his clear handwriting the famous *Rules of Civility.* These maxims were not invented by George, but to a great extent he tried to live by them:

"Labor to keep alive in your Breast that Little Spark of Celestial fire called Conscience.

"Every Action done in Company, ought to be with Some Sign of Respect to those that are Present.

"Keep your Nails clean and Short, also your Hands and Teeth clean . . ."

It should be remembered that Washington was a person who even at an early age understood what it meant to be a gentleman. He was not without flaws in character, some of which took years to overcome. However, he was "cleanly in an age of filth," did not use profanity, was a good host and a pleasant guest, and tried always to be thoughtful and courteous. Some of the rules he was copying obviously were aimed at people far less well-bred than he:

"Spit not in the Fire . . .

"Kill no Vermin as Fleas, lice ticks &c in the Sight of Others . . .

"Mock not nor Jest at anything of Importance . . .

"Utter not base and frivolous things amongst grave and Learn'd Men . . .

"Put not your meat to your Mouth with your Knife in your hand neither Spit forth the Stones of any fruit Pye upon a Dish nor cast anything under the table."

What manners some people must have had!

Meanwhile Washington's copy books and accounts show a growing knowledge of mathematics, legal forms, the sciences of surveying and navigation, and the careful use of money. Sometimes they give us a flash of revelation into the problems of his often-troubled young heart. Occasionally he sat daydreaming, drawing curious little birds upon the margins of his paper. Several times he composed passionately unhappy poems of which we will speak later. There were moments of wonder, of hope, of uncertainty and of brief despair—

emotions which have disturbed young people since the beginning of the world.

However, there are ways to work off such brooding! Young Washington had inherited health from both parents and a strong physique from his father. He wrestled, threw the bar, vaulted with the long pole and raced on foot—outpacing in all these sports most of his friends. His greatest joy, however, was to ride horseback, leaping fences and gullies and racing with the wind. Thomas Jefferson was later to acclaim him the most superb horseman he had ever seen. This is the more remarkable when one considers that Virginia was then, as it still is, famous for its great horses and great riders. Still the boy was restless, wondering whether he should not break completely with his pleasant way of life and go to sea.

His half-brother Lawrence appears to have encouraged him in this ambition (possibly as they sat talking, looking out over the wide Potomac). George must have dreamed of himself as a wealthy captain taking cargoes of tobacco to England and returning with whole argosies of valuable merchandise. Ships' captains were treated with great respect, and they were their own masters on land or on sea. Perhaps George did not realize the hazards of such a life or the long-hard climb from cab-in boy to captain.

There is a tradition that he had his sea chest packed when Mary Ball Washington made her final decision, putting an end to his seagoing dreams. He was her oldest son, the man of the family since his father's death. He would not be allowed to throw his life away in such a manner. Silently George obeyed. But in his heart he knew that some day soon he must start making his own decisions.

CHAPTER 4

COMPASS NEEDLE AND CUPID'S DART

WHEN GEORGE WASHINGTON WAS SIXTEEN HE WENT to live with his brother Lawrence at Mount Vernon. Situated on a bluff above the Potomac, it was within sight of Belvoir, the plantation house of the Fairfaxes not far down the river.

Lord Fairfax, the wealthy head of this clan, had but recently arrived from England. This English gentleman, who was to play an important part in George's life during the next few years, was one of the greatest landowners in the world. From his mother he had inherited the fabulous Culpeper Grant, a royal gift from King Charles II, which included every acre of the "Northern Neck" of Virginia—all the land lying between the Rappahannock and the Potomac rivers seaward from the Blue Ridge Mountains. Fairfax believed that the grant also gave him possession of the land between those streams to their remote head-waters or "first fountains." He therefore laid claim to more than five million acres, much of it beyond the Blue Ridge and including most of the beautiful valley of the Shenandoah.

Colonel William Fairfax, a cousin of the English owner, had been appointed the Virginia land agent for all this property. It was William who had built Belvoir, to which Lord Fairfax came as a guest upon his arrival in America.

Colonel Fairfax was the father of Nancy, who had recently become the bride of Lawrence Washington. He also had a son, George William, who had been schooled in England. Although George William Fairfax was seven years older than George Washington they soon became close friends—a friendship which was to last for many years.

George Washington shared the hospitable ties between these two houses, rode to hounds with old Lord Fairfax, and gratefully accepted his guidance in the choice of books and periodicals. He attended balls and other entertainments at Belvoir, played cards and billiards with these neighbors, and sometimes visited them for weeks at a time, bringing as many as nine clean shirts and six linen waistcoats, and not forgetting his razor—a proud new acquisition.

It may have been at about this time that Mary Washington asked Lord Fairfax's advice concerning her oldest son. Fairfax is said to have written in reply:

> *Honored Madam*: You are so good as to ask what I think of a temporary residence for your son George in England. It is a country for which I myself have no inclination, and the gentlemen you mention are certainly renowned gamblers and rakes, which I should be sorry your son were exposed to, even if his means easily admitted of a residence in England. He is strong and hardy, and as good a master of a horse as any could desire. His education might have been bettered, but what he has is accurate and inclines him to much life out of doors. He is very grave for one of his age, and reserved in his intercourse; not a great talker at any time. His mind appears to me to act slowly, but, on the whole, to reach just conclusions, and he has an ardent wish to see the right of questions—what my friend Mr. Addison was pleased to call "the intellectual conscience." Method and exactness seem to be

natural to George. He is, I suspect, beginning to feel the sap rising, being in the spring of life, and is getting ready to be the prey of your sex, wherefore may the Lord help him, and deliver him from the nets those spiders, called women, will cast for his ruin. I presume him to be truthful because he is exact. I wish I could say that he governs his temper. He is subject to attacks of anger on provocation, and sometimes without just cause; but as he is a reasonable person, time will cure him of this vice of nature, and in fact he is, in my judgement, a man who will go to school all his life and profit thereby.

I hope, madam, that you will find pleasure in what I have written, and will rest assured that I shall continue to interest myself in his fortunes.

Much honored by your appeal to my judgement, I am, my dear madam, your obedient humble servant.

FAIRFAX

Lord Fairfax did continue to interest himself in his young neighbor, and in a mutually profitable way. Fairfax knew that if he were to maintain his claim to his lands beyond the Blue Ridge they must be surveyed. And in George he had a fine young surveyor ready for the task.

Although many Americans know that George Washington was an accomplished surveyor, few but scholars seem to realize how early he acquired this science and how widely he practiced it. From his fourteenth year on we have, in his own precise hand, maps of his survey, sometimes handsomely decorated with a compass or other embellishments. He surveyed his birthplace at Pope's Creek, Ferry Farm on the Rappahannock and Mount Vernon time and again. He laid out the town of Belhaven (now Alexandria, Virginia) and for another fifty years was "running off" lots, farms and fortifications—in all "more than 200 tracts containing upward of 66,000 acres." Deeply interested not only in surveying, but in purchasing fertile land, George must have been well aware of the opportunity being offered him by Lord Fairfax. Now he had a chance to earn as much as a doubloon a day (worth about $7.20) and to see Fairfax's vast frontier domain in the Shenandoah Valley. George William Fairfax and another older surveyor would be in charge of the party. But Washington would be an important and busy assistant.

Here in 1748 begin the *Diaries of George Washington.* And this is his first entry:

> *Fryday March 11th. . . .*
> Began my journey in Company with George (William) Fairfax, Esqr., we travell'd this day 40 Miles . . .

29

During the next half century Washington would travel from Maine to Georgia, and from the Eastern seaboard to the confluence of the Kanawha and the Ohio rivers (now Point Pleasant, West Virginia). He would know at first hand more about his country than any other man then alive. But now we see him at the age of sixteen heading into the wilderness on his first surveying expedition for Lord Fairfax.

On the second day they crossed the Blue Ridge Mountains at Ashby's Gap, where they must have had a breathtaking view of the Shenandoah Valley spread out below them, the river itself twisting like a silver snake through the still-leafless forests of March. However, George Washington's only comment was: "Nothing remarkable happen'd."

The following day's entry shows more enthusiasm:

> Rode to his Lordships Quarter about 4 Miles higher up the River we went through most beautiful Groves of Sugar Trees and spent the best part of the Day in admiring the Trees and richness of the Land.

This was to be the site of the future Greenway Court, Lord Fairfax's rambling wilderness mansion and his residence after 1749. Obviously George Washington approved of his Lordship's choice of land.

Muddy trails, swollen rivers, vermin-infested beds and much hard work faced these young surveyors. But George Washington, after his first amazement, proved capable of facing all hardships. For instance, on his fifth night away from the clean sheets and comfortable beds of Mount Vernon, he found himself under "one thread Bear blanket with double its Weight of Vermin," but he survived the ordeal.

The surveyors found the Potomac flooded by great rains in the mountains and they traveled "the worst Road that ever was trod by Man or Beast." Once they ran completely out of food. On another occasion "our Plates was a Large Chip as for Dishes we had none." One night the straw on which they were sleeping caught fire. Sometimes they had to leave their tent because it was "so Intolerable smoky." On still another "blostering night" the tent was carried quite away by the wind.

But George Washington was having the time of his life despite these discomforts. He and his party shot wild turkeys for food. They managed to survey many tracts of fertile land. Perhaps the most entertaining moment of the trip was when they were "agreeably surprised at the sight of thirty odd Indians coming from War with only one Scalp."

They induced these Indians to perform a "War Daunce" around a big fire. "... the best Dauncer jumps up as one awaked out of a sleep and runs and Jumps about the Ring in a most comical Manner." George was fascinated by the "Musick" produced by such instruments as "a Pot half (full) of Water with a Deerskin Stretched over it as tight as it can and a goard with some Shott in it to Rattle and a Piece of an horses Tail tied to it to make it look fine." One Indian was rattling, another drumming and all the rest "Dauncing." (It is obvious that George Washington was learning more about surveying and Indian customs than about spelling and grammar!)

The last entry breathes a sigh of relief. "*Wednesday the 13th of April 1748* Mr. Fairfax got safe home and I myself safe to my Brothers which concludes my Journal."

But although George was safe from flood and fire and "Dauncing" Indians, he was not safe from the disturbingly beautiful girls of the Tidewater!

George Washington was in love with one girl after

another during his youth, but for some reason he was unsuccessful in all these early courtships. He was probably shy and awkward in the presence of Tidewater belles. He was never to become a fluent conversationalist, had not been educated in England and, comparatively speaking, was a poor young man. In fact he was not a particularly good "catch"—and the Virginia girls let him realize it.

This made him so miserable that he wrote at least two unhappy love poems in a perfect welter of bad grammar and emotional tumult. These poems make him seem far from the statuesque and wooden figure of the Stuart portraits or of the Weems' fables. In fact, they reveal a most human and even pitiable young man. He must have fallen in love with a Frances Alexander in his mid-teens, for at about this time he wrote the following lines in which the first letters spell FRANCES ALEXA . . . :

From your bright sparkling Eyes, I was undone;
Rays, you have; more transparent than the sun,
A midst its glory in the rising Day,
None can you equal in your bright array;
Constant in your calm and unspotted Mind;
Cqual to all, but will to none Prove king,
So Knowing, seldom one so Young, you'l Find.

Ah! woes me, that I should love and conceal,
Long have I wish'd, but never dare reveal
Even though severly Loves Pains I feel;
Xerxes that great, was't free from Cupid's Dart,
And all the greatest Heroes, felt the smart.

It will be noticed that even so brave a young man as Washington quailed before the challenge of four additional lines beginning with N-D-E-R to complete ALEXANDER!

But Frances was not the only Tidewater flirt who was then or later to pierce Washington's heart with Cupid's rhyming dart.

Some other girl may have driven the desperate youthful poet to attempt the following agonized verse, which begins:

Oh Ye Gods why should my Poor Resistless Heart
Stand to oppose thy might and Power
At Last surrender to cupid's feather'd Dart
And now lays Bleeding every Hour. . . .

Who could this pitiless girl be? Perhaps she was the mysterious charmer whom Washington called his "Lowland Beauty." She is still unidentified, although many Tidewater families now claim kinship.

Perhaps the girl was Betsy Fauntleroy, who had kept George dangling for three long years. Perhaps she was Lucy Grymes, who later became the wife of Henry Lee, the mother of Lighthorse Harry Lee, and the grandmother of Robert E. Lee.

Possibly she was one of the two Cary sisters at Belvoir. Mary Cary was slightly younger than George. Sally, married to George William Fairfax, was slightly older. George Washington was for a time deeply in love with the wife of his best friend, easily the most entrancing woman he had ever met. However, not a breath of scandal has come down from that age of gossip concerning George Washington and Sally Cary Fairfax. Both realized that nothing could come of such a love but unhappiness for all concerned.

However, among the other girls he courted, there must have been several who in later years wondered why they had been so cool and calculating in refusing the hand of the young man who was soon to become Virginia's greatest hero.

CHAPTER 5

SEA VOYAGE
TO BARBADOS

MEANWHILE, LAWRENCE WASHINGTON HAD DEVELOPED a racking cough with apparent symptoms of tuberculosis. It had become impossible for this conscientious man to carry on his many duties as Burgess, Adjutant of the Virginia military forces, master of Mount Vernon and official of the Ohio Company. The latter was the project of an ambitious group seeking profit in frontier lands and trade with the Indians.

George had twice accompanied his brother to a rude frontier health resort where the waters of the warm springs had done little to remedy Lawrence's failing health. Now this beloved older brother asked the young surveyor to take a voyage with him to Barbados, an island famed for its healthful climate. Lawrence's wife Nancy, now caring for a ten-month-old infant, obviously could not risk the rough sea voyage.

Late in September, 1751, the ship on which they were taking passage dropped down the Potomac River into Chesapeake Bay and sailed southward through the Atlantic, bound for Bridgetown, Barbados.

This was George Washington's first and last salt-water journey. The boy who had longed to go to sea, and who had studied navigation, began to keep a "log" of the trip which would have done justice to a junior officer of the vessel.

For this journal he ruled his paper like a log book and each day entered the course of the ship, its speed and the direction and force of the wind. In fact his diaries for many years would be concerned with the state of the weather.

Like an old salt, he speaks of reefing sail or crowding on all sail, of smooth seas, moderate breezes, brisker wind, hard squalls of wind and rain, and such near-hurricanes that the seaman confessed "they had never seen such weather before." But not until the return voyage did

George Washington experience even a moment of seasickness. The reader concludes that he might, indeed, have become a good sea captain.

In pleasant weather they fished, managing on one lucky day to catch a dolphin, a shark and a pilot fish—the first and last of which were dressed and cooked for dinner.

George must have had the leisure during these thirty-three days at sea to take stock of his life and perhaps to attempt to look into the misty future. Behind him lay three years of hard work as a surveyor. He had religiously saved his earnings and invested them in land far more fertile than any he had inherited. It is true that every girl he had asked had declined to marry him. But one of these days, he promised himself, he would be a wealthy and successful plantation owner, and possibly even a Burgess and an officer of the Virginia forces. If George regretted the months of profitable work he was missing by accompanying his brother to Barbados, he does not mention the fact in his journal.

On the second of November they were "alarmed" by the cry of "Land." It was four in the morning when "we quitted our beds with surprise," finding the island clearly visible.

George Washington's affection and concern for his sick brother is indicated by the fact that he does not so much as mention the beauties of Barbados before reporting upon an examination of Lawrence made by a famous local physician. Dr. William Hillary gave his professional opinion that "a cure might be effectually made." Relieved by this good news, George lets himself note that this blossoming island appeared "perfectly ravishing" with field of "Cain, Corn, Fruit Trees, &c in a delightful Green."

Situated in a handsome rented house on a hillside overlooking Carlyle Bay, the Virginia visitors were soon made aware of the island's hospitality.

Major Clarke entertained them at "the Club call'd Beefstake and Tripe." They were "Genteely receiv'd by Judge Satuo Maynard and Lady and agreeably entertain'd by the Company . . . After Dinner was the greatest Collection of Fruits I have yet seen on the Table." On November 13th they "Dined at the Fort with some Ladys." And they went to a play, perhaps the first George Washington had ever seen, about which he writes cautiously in his journal, "the character of Barnwell and several others was said to be well performed."

All this might have gone on happily for weeks, save for

the fact that the healthful climate of Barbados was not living up to its reputation. Lawrence became so ill that he could not leave their lodgings. Then it was George's turn to be endangered. Between November 17th and December 12th there is but one entry in his journal: "Was strongly attacked with the small Pox: sent for Dr. Lanahan whose attendance was very constant till my recovery and going out, which as not 'till Thursday the 12th of December.

History would have been sadly changed if that terrible scourge of the 18th century had carried off George Washington as it often did whole families and villages. Fortunately he was not so deeply pock-marked as some victims, and now he had an immunity which would be of great advantage to him in the years to come. But it should be noted that throughout this ordeal Washington confided to his journal not one word of complaint.

It was now evident that the island's climate was proving to be no benefit to Lawrence's tuberculosis. Presumably the brothers held a council of war, deciding that George would return to Virginia while Lawrence would sail directly to Bermuda, still in search of his vanishing health. If Bermuda proved curative, Lawrence would write to George who would then accompany Lawrence's wife

Nancy and their child to Bermuda. Always sweetly agreeable to anything Lawrence requested, George began to prepare for the homeward journey.

Aboard ship once again, George had time to comment on the luxuriant island he was leaving. He saw this West Indian island as "one entire fortification" defended by entrenchments, guns and a well-disciplined militia. But he also saw it as a fertile garden spot and could not understand how planters living on such rich land could find themselves in financial trouble. His two most compelling life interests, farming and military matters, are apparent in this keen report upon Barbados.

Three days out of Bridgeport, the ship celebrated Christmas. Washington's journal entry for December 25, 1751, calls the day "fine and clear and pleasant with moderate sea." They dined on an "Irish goose" fattened for the occasion and "drank a health to our absent friends." After rough weather they passed the Capes into Chesapeake Bay, and entered the mouth of the York River on January 26th, 1752.

George Washington hurried on to Williamsburg, the capital of colonial Virginia, where he met Governor Robert Dinwiddie, who was soon to play such an important and sometimes aggravating role in his life. George was evidently bringing letters from Lawrence, a man of importance in the Governor's eyes. He was "received Graceously" by Dinwiddie who inquired as to Lawrence's health and asked George to stay to dine.

By February 2nd Washington was on his way to Mount Vernon by way of Pope's Creek and Ferry Farm. It must have been with more sadness than home-coming joy that this bearer of bad tidings dismounted before the mansion house he loved, mulling over in his mind how best to tell Nancy the disturbing news about her husband.

Nancy and George never did make that trip to Bermuda. Lawrence's health grew steadily worse and he soon hastened home to say farewell to his wife and little daughter. Still brave as always, and thoughtful of those he was leaving behind, he labored over his elaborate last will and testament until three days before his death. He was buried in the vault at Mount Vernon where nearly half a century later the body of George was also to be laid. So these two half-brothers, more like father and son to each other, were to remain close even in death.

It had been George's father's wish that Mount Vernon

should become the property of George if Lawrence had no living offspring to inherit it. In a complicated and not entirely clear document, Lawrence made a somewhat similar provision in favor of his "beloved brother George"—first taking care of his widow's life-interest.

When Nancy's baby daughter died, thus removing any possible "heir of the flesh," and when Nancy remarried and moved to Westmoreland, Mount Vernon came to George Washington. However, he paid Lawrence's widow 15,000 pounds of tobacco in rent each year for nearly a decade. When, in time, Nancy and her second husband died, there was no one alive save George with even the remotest claim upon Mount Vernon, that beloved country seat which Washington had been surveying and re-surveying since his fifteenth year. Until the very year of his death he would be improving and remodeling it. Here was the peaceful home above the "River of Swans" which would never leave his thoughts through the dark hours of two wars which lay ahead.

CHAPTER 6

DANGER ON THE OHIO FRONTIER

WE SOMETIMES FORGET THAT AMERICA MIGHT WELL have been a French-speaking nation. By the year 1535 the French explorer Jacques Cartier had sailed up the St. Lawrence to the present site of Montreal. For more than two centuries it was the French who had the easiest access to the interior by way of the St. Lawrence River and the Great Lakes. Meanwhile the English were hemmed in on the coastal plain along the Atlantic by the formidable Appalachian Mountains.

England and France, traditional enemies in Europe, continued their struggle in the North American wilderness. Each time these great nations went to war in Europe there was bloodshed, scalping and burning on the American frontier. And even when no war was in progress the two rival powers maneuvered to gain the friendship of various Indian tribes and thus a larger percentage of the lucrative trade in beaver skins.

Not until Washington was a young man, however, did the French and the English clash on the remote Ohio River. When English-speaking fur traders from Pennsylvania and Virginia began to penetrate the Appalachians, the French were seriously alarmed. They realized that unless they could hold the Fork of the Ohio (where the Monongahela and the Allegheny rivers join to form the larger stream) the English would soon have control of the whole Ohio River valley.

The French king and his ministers therefore decided to send troops to build a fort at the spot where Pittsburgh now stands. And the English king, hearing of the new French penetration, sent a message to Governor Dinwiddie of Virginia telling him to prevent the French from accomplishing any such move—by force of arms if necessary.

In the autumn of 1753 young George Washington, who

had but recently been appointed an Adjutant of the Virginia forces, was summoned to Williamsburg by Governor Dinwiddie. The Governor explained that a previous messenger sent to warn the French on the Ohio had failed in his mission. The Governor asked George if he would be willing to undertake the difficult and dangerous task of traveling hundreds of miles through the uncharted wilderness in late autumn and early winter to warn off the French.

How speedily Washington complied is told in the excellent journal he kept of his trip. He says that he "set out on the intended Journey the same day." At Fredericksburg he picked up a French-speaking former Dutch soldier named Van Braam whose limited knowledge of French would, on a later expedition, prove very embarrassing to Washington. At Alexandria he purchased many needed supplies. At Winchester in the Shenandoah Valley he acquired baggage and horses and soon was headed up the rough trail to Wills Creek (now Cumberland, Maryland).

The flaming leaves and blue skies of October had changed to the rain-sodden dreariness of November before Major Washington reached Wills Creek. This was the deepest he had ever penetrated into the mountainous wilderness to the westward. Luckily Christopher Gist, the famous frontiersman whom Dinwiddie has suggested as a guide, was at home when Washington arrived.

Here at Wills Creek Washington hired four "servitors" to handle the horses and the baggage. Then these men, plus the Major, Gist and Van Braam, began their struggle over the Allegheny Mountains, Laurel Ridge and the other great hills that lay between them and the Fork of the Ohio. Up and up they labored to rock ledges which seemed to be the top of the world, their hearts beating with struggle, their breath white on the frosty air. Here was exciting country George had never previously seen—and great adventure lay just ahead. The stakes for which the English and French were playing were almost beyond imagination. Although George Washington may not have realized it, the two great colonial powers were fighting not only for the fur trade, but for the North American continent as well.

Christopher Gist, a brave, dependable and educated man, knew the country well, and doubtless proved more than a mere guide on this mission. As they sat roasting venison over the campfire at night, he probably told young

Major Washington what to expect in difficult conferences with the Indians which lay just ahead.

Neither side in this struggle could hope to win unless they could obtain and hold the friendship of Indian allies. These were undependable partners at best. The English believed, however, that they could count upon the traditional friendship of the Six Nations—the Iroquois Federation—which had long been at odds with the French. They also hoped they could trust the Delaware and Shawnee tribes on the Ohio.

The most powerful single figure among the Ohio Indians was Half King, so called because he also held allegiance to the Iroquois. As Christopher Gist doubtless explained, Half King was furious with the French. They had, he said, "killed and eaten" his father, and were now threatening to oust his tribesmen from their ancient hunting grounds.

Half King had already visited the French Commandant, Sieur de Marin, who had received him rudely. Half King thereupon had made a brave and dignified speech warning the French. He had said:

"If you had come in a peaceful Manner, like our Brothers, the *English*, we should not have been against you trading with us, as they do; but to come, Fathers, and build houses upon our land, and to take it by force, is what we cannot submit to."

Half King said that the land belonged to neither the English nor the French. "The Great Being above" had given it as a place for the Indians to reside. He said that the two white nations now claiming the land were on trial "to see which will have the greatest Regard" for justice and right. He had told the French Commandant that he and his Indians would be allied with the side which proved itself honorable in this trial and would fight the other, "for I am not afraid to discharge you off this Land."

The brusque and very rude French General, who had brought soldiers to seize the Ohio country, was reported to have replied to the dignified old chieftain:

"Now, my child, I have heard your Speech . . . I am not afraid of Flies or Mosquitoes, for *Indians* are such as those. I tell you, down the River I will go, and will build upon it, according to my command. If the River was block'd up, I have forces sufficient to burst it open and tread under my Feet all that Stand in Opposition, together with their Alliances; for my Force is as the Sand upon the Sea Shore; therefore, here is your Wampum, I fling it at you."

Those were fighting words for a French general to throw at the strongest Indian chief of the region, a warrior who already hated the French. And Washington was happy to report all these colorful insults in the concise and informative journal which he would prepare from his rough notes upon his return. Certainly the young Major had reason to hope that Half King's well-motivated hatred against the French would not cool as the Virginians labored toward that chieftain's native haunts over icy ridges and windswept valleys.

On November 22nd Washington and his party reached the post kept by the Indian trader and gunsmith John Frazier, located at the mouth of Turtle Creek where it enters the Monongahela River. Frazier had no love for the French, who had recently evicted him from his home and trading post on the Allegheny at Venango (now Franklin, Pennsylvania). He was eager to tell Washington all of the latest news. Three tribes of "French Indians" were on the warpath against the English. The French Commandant, Sieur de Marin, who had been so rude to Half King, now was dead, and the greater part of the French forces had withdrawn northward for the winter. Frazier naturally wished the young Virginia Major all success on his mission.

George Washington realized that winter was at hand. He was therefore eager to push on to the Fork of the Ohio where the quiet and deep-flowing Monongahela meets the more turbulent Allegheny to become the Ohio River. With his keen engineering eye he realized that here at the Fork was land "extremely well situated for a Fort, as it has the absolute Command of both Rivers." The notes in his journal concerning the strategic value of the present site of Pittsburgh give us one of our first glimpses of his potential military genius.

At Logs Town, not far down the Ohio, Washington had the good fortune to discover and hire an excellent Indian interpreter, John Davison. And it was here that he held conferences with famous Half King, Monakotoocha, the later-traitorous Shingiss, old Jeskakake, White Thunder and other chieftains. Half King had been summoned from his hunting cabin. When he arrived, Washington interviewed the great chief privately in his tent with only Davison, the interpreter, present. And it was at this interview that Washington learned even more about the rude treatment Half King had suffered from the late French Commandant. Washington told Half King that he, Washington, had been sent by the Governor of Virginia to give a message to the French. He asked directions to the French forts to the north. Half King was eager to give him every possible aid, including the promise of a party of Indians to guide him.

However, there now began a series of exasperating delays. Half King must call in and consult other chiefs of the Shawnees and Delawares. He must gather the wampum belts given as tokens of peace between the French and Indians. These he must secure to throw in anger at the feet of the French. It was a very important matter, this breaking with their Fathers, the French, to join their Brothers, the English. And Half King, loyal though he was to the English, was not to be hurried.

Meanwhile news came that the French were again warning the Indians, threatening that in the spring they would descend the river in great numbers. They boasted that they would "fight the *English* three years . . ." and would conquer. Already Washington was aware that the wily French had lured to their side many tribes who any day might begin raiding the Pennsylvania-Virginia frontier. With the weather worsening, each delay now seemed insupportable. But young Major Washington knew he must not offend Half King by appearing hasty.

At last Half King, Jeskakake and White Thunder, bearing the wampum belts to be returned to the French, set out with Washington and his party on the way to the French Command, by way of Venango. Also accompanying them was a single Indian hunter to kill wild game for their food.

The weather was deplorable, and all the streams were flooded, but on December 4th they reached Venango. There Washington very wisely established the Indians in camp, himself proceeding to the outpost. "We found the *French* Colours hoisted at a House from which they had driven Mr. *John Frazier*, an *English* Subject." One captures the note of excitement and subdued anger in Washington's journal as he stepped at last into the enemy camp on territory "rightfully belonging" to his Master, the King of England.

Three officers at this house, including the famous half-breed, Captain Joncaire, greeted Washington and his party most courteously and invited them to dinner; an invitation which the polished young gentleman from Tidewater Virginia accepted willingly.

Captain Joncaire informed Washington that he himself was in command of the Ohio. But when Washington tried to deliver Governor Dinwiddie's message, the Captain told him of "a General Officer at the near Fort" where he must now proceed to apply for an answer.

At dinner there was wine. ". . . As they (the French) dosed themselves pretty plentifully with it," Washington wrote, it soon "banished the Restraint which at first appeared in their Conversation; and gave a licence to the Tongues to reveal their Sentiments more freely. They told me, That it was their absolute Design to take Possession of the *Ohio*, and by G— they would do it."

Here was evidence enough that the French meant business. Washington became increasingly impatient to deliver his message and to return to Virginia. He cleverly drew out Joncaire and the two other French officers until he had rather complete knowledge of all the French forts between Venango and Montreal, plus facts concerning the stores and soldiers at each stronghold.

But if Washington, sober, knew how to draw out slightly inebriated Frenchmen, those Frenchmen even in their cups knew how to deal with Indians. Here at Venango and later at Fort Le Boeuf the French plied the chiefs liberally with liquor, slyly refused them conference in which they might return their wampum belts, made them innumerable promises, delayed them (thus delaying Washington) and otherwise taxed the ingenuity and patience of the young Major. He had come to deliver a message, but now found himself fighting a life and death battle to hold England's Indian allies.

"Rains, Snows and bad Travelling, through many Mires and Swamps" marked the trip to Fort LeBoeuf which was finally sighted on December 11th. Here Washington found in command a dignified silver-haired officer with one eye. This Commandant, Le gardeur de St. Pierre, had "much the air of a Soldier. He was sent over to take the command immediately upon the Death of the late General." After a brief delay Washington was allowed to deliver his letter from Governor Dinwiddie. And while the French officers retired to translate it, Washington took a penetrating look at Fort LeBoeuf. He wrote in his journal:

> .... Four houses compose the Sides. The Bastions are made of Piles driven into the Ground, standing more than 12 feet above it, and sharp at Top: With Port-Holes cut for Cannon, and Loop-Holes for the small Arms to fire through. There are eight *6lb* Pieces mounted, in each Bastion; ... In the Bastions are a Guard-House, Chapel, Doctor's Lodging, and the Commander's private Store.

Military intelligence of first-rate importance! And rare reporting! Meanwhile, at Washington's suggestion, his men were counting the canoes to attempt to determine how large a force the French hoped to transport to the Ohio in the spring. The number of canoes was rather startling: ". . . 50 of Birch Bark, and 170 of Pine; besides many others which were blocked-out, in Readiness to make."

Governor Dinwiddie's courteous but firm message to the French, in the name of his Master, the King of England, was a demand that they remove themselves from English soil. The French General answered in equally courteous terms. In the name of his Master, the King of France, he said he had no intention of complying. Washington now urged the Indian Chief Half King to return the French speech belts, thus breaking all ties with the French, and to prepare for the return journey. However the Commandant, so very courteous to Washington, was even wilier than Joncaire in his use of liquor, flattery and promises of presents to the Indians. He wished to delay the chiefs until after Washington's departure so that he could lure them back as allies.

Washington's journal tells the story:

> December 15*th* The Commandant ordered a plentiful Store of Liquor, Provisions, &c., to be put on Board our Canoe; and appeared to be extremely complaisant, though he was exerting every Artifice which he could invent to set our own *Indians* at Variance with us, to prevent their going 'till after our Departure. Presents, Rewards, and every Thing which could be suggested by him or his Officers—I can't say that ever in my Life I suffered so much Anxiety as I did in this Affair: I saw that every Stratagem which the most fruitful Brain could invent was practiced, to win the Half-King to their Interest."

Major Washington, who never before had set forth on a diplomatic mission, was learning swiftly the elaborate diplomacy of both the Indians and the French. It must be said to his everlasting credit that through straightforward appeals to both the Indians and the French, plus certain wiles of his own, he managed to bring the Indians away by canoe in one of their few sober moments, and to leave the French with little satisfaction as to the success of their counter diplomacy.

The return journey was a nightmare of flooded streams, floating ice, and deep snow through which they floundered. The horses, which had been sent ahead, were overtaken. But these poor beasts were so feeble and exhausted that "myself and others . . . gave up our Horses for Packs, to assist along with the Baggage . . . and continued with them three Days, till I found there was no Probability of their getting home in any reasonable time."

Washington, in buckskin shirt and leggings, now suggested that he and his guide, Christopher Gist, leave Van Braam and the others to follow more slowly with the horses, while they themselves hastened forward on foot.

Gist knew the severity of the weather and the difficulties of walking hundreds of weary miles through deep snow. He tried to dissuade the impetuous young Major. But Washington, aware that his information might save the Ohio from the invading French, insisted upon his bold plan. This young Virginia gentleman who had always traveled on horseback and never on foot now marched off bravely toward the Fork of the Ohio through cold so intense that even he admitted it was "scarcely supportable."

Near a miserable village appropriately named "Murdering Town" they met an Indian who hailed Gist by his Indian name, professing to be an old acquaintance. Gist believed he had previously seen this skulking savage at Joncaire's outpost, and realized that he might be sympathetic to the French. However, when the Indian offered to show them the nearest way to the Fork of the Ohio they accepted his guidance.

After leading them for several miles through the silent forest, the Indian suddenly wheeled, took aim and fired point-blank at the white men behind him. George cried to Gist, "Are you shot?" But fortunately neither was touched by the bullet.

Leaping ahead and taking shelter behind a tree, the Indian began frantically reloading his gun. However, in that instant the two men were upon him. Gist was for killing him immediately. George mercifully insisted upon sparing him—a very humane but dangerous decision there in the wilderness.

Dismissing the Indian, who was doubtless thankful for his life, Washington and Gist walked all that night and all the next day to avoid what now seemed a well-laid French plot to ambush and destroy them. At last they reached the Allegheny River, a stream they must cross on their homeward journey.

Washington records in his journal:

> We expected to have found the River frozen, but it
> was not, only about 50 Yards from each Shore; The Ice
> I suppose had broke up above, for it was driving in vast
> Quantities.
>
> There was no Way for getting over but on a Raft;
> Which we set about with but one poor Hachet, and
> finished just before Sunsetting. This was a whole Day's
> Work. Then set off; But before we were Half Way over,
> we were jammed in the Ice, in such a Manner that we
> expected every Moment our Raft to sink, and ourselves
> to perish. I put out my setting Pole to try to stop the Raft,
> that the Ice might pass by; when the Rapidity of the
> Stream threw it with so much violence against the Pole,
> that it jerked me out into ten Feet Water; but I
> fortunately saved myself by catching hold of one of the
> Raft Logs.

They could not get across that night. But they did reach
a barren island where they lay, freezing and soaked, all
through the hours of darkness.

> The Cold was so extremely severe, that Mr. *Gist*
> had all his Fingers and some of his Toes frozen; but the
> Water was shut up so hard, that we found no Difficulty
> in getting off the Island, on the Ice, in the Morning, and
> went to Mr. Frazier's.

Here were warmth, food and much-needed horses and
provisions for the trails ahead.

Washington, still trying to bolster Virginia's Indian alliances, gave a warm coat to the important Indian chieftainess, Queen Aliquippa of the Delaware Nation, who lived not far away. Then, pressing homeward on horseback, he labored once again through all those snowy mountains toward the Tidewater. He stopped briefly at Belvoir for a night's rest. Next morning he hastened on to Williamsburg. He arrived there on January 16th, having covered many hundreds of miles through the bleak wilderness, and having accomplished his perilous mission in two and one-half adventuresome and never-to-be-forgotten months.

The Governor gave Washington just one day in which to prepare his report. This was rushed to the printers to appear as the famous Journal frequently quoted in this chapter, a clear warning which startled Virginia and England into preparing their neglected defenses for what would soon become the bloody French and Indian War.

CHAPTER 7

FIRST VICTORY AND FIRST DEFEAT

GOVERNOR DINWIDDIE AND HIS YOUNG ADJUTANT-COURIER were of a single mind concerning the French threat to the Fork of the Ohio. Troops must be raised and equipped immediately and a force dispatched strong enough to evict the enemy. The twenty-two-year-old George, who had never experienced a single day of soldiering in his entire life, was sufficiently modest to say that he did not expect supreme command of the expedition. ". . . for I must be impartial enough to confess, it is a charge too great for my youth and inexperience to be entrusted with."

He did hope, however, that he might be promoted to the

rank of lieutenant-colonel and be placed second in command. In this he was not disappointed.

From the first week of his new commission, young Washington was put severely to the test. The Virginia House of Burgesses was reluctant to vote necessary funds. And few Virginians of military age were eager to enlist for a campaign so difficult at such small pay.

Early in March, Washington wrote from Alexandria to Governor Dinwiddie:

> We daily Experience the great necessity for Cloathing the Men, as we find the generality . . . are . . . loose, Idle Persons, that are quite destitute of House, and Home . . . many of them without Shoes, others want stockings, some are without Shirts, and not a few that have Scarce a Coat or Waistcoat to their backs . . .

In addition there were few officers of any rank to undertake the training of these "self-willed, ungovernable people."

Governor Dinwiddie had chosen a former mathematics professor at William and Mary College, a much respected gentleman named Joshua Fry, as colonel of the regiment. However, since the Colonel was never with the forward troops, Washington was at all times in effective command.

Under Washington were Major George Muse, Captain Adam Stephen, Captain Peter Hog, and a scattering of other officers, virtually all untrained in their profession. To bolster his staff, Washington requested that his companion of the previous winter, Jacob Van Braam, be commissioned. This was a generous gesture which later he would have reason to regret.

The French would have smiled could they have seen that small force of raw recruits leaving Alexandria on April 2, 1754, to follow their brave but completely inexperienced commander, Lieutenant-Colonel George Washington of the Virginia Militia, astride his spirited horse. No greener contingent of half-trained civilians ever ventured out to defend a continent. It required seven painful days to march these men the first seventy-four muddy miles to Winchester in the Shenandoah Valley. There Captain Adam Stephen had raised just enough additional recruits to make Washington's total command 159 reluctant volunteers.

These colonial armies were always shy of transport. Washington tried to "impress" (that is, legally seize and pay for) seventy-four wagons. After laboring for a week at this task he had rounded up but ten, "and some of those so badly provided with teams that the soldiers were obliged to assist them up the hills."

By the time this little expedition reached Wills Creek, jumping-off place for the heroic struggle through the mountains, news came that the French had seized the Fork of the Ohio. They had driven off a small construction party of Virginians sent out in advance to build a fort at this point. Washington wrote Dinwiddie the disconcerting information that the French, rumored at upward of 1,000, had eighteen pieces of cannon and numerous Indian allies.

Thus the enemy could muster perhaps six times as many soldiers as Washington. They were already in possession of the strategic Fork of the Ohio, and were busily engaged in building a strong fort, complete withartillery. They had an excellent line of communication, mostly by water. And their soldiers were trained fighting men.

Lieutenant-Colonel Washington, by contrast, had very poor transport, few supplies and no such array of cannon. Ahead of him lay many miles of unbroken forest, tilting skyward in a succession of heartbreaking mountain ridges. Nevertheless, despite all the odds against him, he was determined to fight.

He first called a council of war with his small staff of officers. Then he wrote to Governor Dinwiddie:

> Your Honor will see . . . that I am destined to the Monongahela with all the diligent dispatch in my power. We will endeavor to make the road sufficiently good for the heaviest artillery to pass, and when we arrive at Redstone Creek, fortify ourselves as strongly as the short time will allow.

Any motorist who now speeds along Route 40 to the west of Cumberland, Maryland, will have slight conception of the immense difficulties facing the young Lieutenant-Colonel struggling at about three miles a day through that eighteenth-century wilderness. Sweating axmen labored to clear the brush and trees from the steep slopes of the precipitous ridges. Boulders were moved, streams were crudely bridged where the water was too deep to ford. Then straining horses, aided by exhausted men, pulled the vehicles up the rough mountain sides through the Indian-haunted forests.

Despite pleas for help dispatched to several colonial governors, there were at first no troops except the Virginians moving against the French at Fort Duquesne. And when at long last a single "Independent Company" from South Carolina under a certain Captain Mackay overtook Washington's little army, any joy the Virginians might have felt at this reinfor-cement soon disappeared. These proud South Carolinians were not colonial militia. They were part of the British military establishment. As "regulars," these troops of His Majesty were not only better paid, better dressed and better fed than Washington's colonials, but felt them-selves above any such lowly labor as helping to build the road. Adding insult to injury, Captain Mackay refused to take orders from Lieutenant-Colonel Washington, claiming superior rights and privileges as an officer of His Majesty's troops.

Washington then and later was incensed by this ridiculous and dangerous distinction between colonial and royal forces. At one point his Virginia officers were on the verge of mutiny. Washington himself protested vigorously in a letter to Governor Dinwiddie. But the cautious and complacent Governor did nothing to appease Washington or to correct an ugly situation.

To a less brave or a more experienced commander the expedition might often have appeared hopeless. Food was short, morale was poor, and little help was forthcoming from Virginia's typically undependable Indian allies. Now came rumors that the French were moving against him in considerable numbers. Washington might well have been forgiven for ordering a strategic retreat. But he gave no such order.

His meager force was now moving through the low and rolling hills of the wide and wooded valley between Laurel Hill and Chestnut Ridge. Here the young officer decided to defend himself as best he could.

Many critics have since pointed out that Washington showed no particular military genius in choosing the location of Fort Necessity. The site was a marshy swale at the confluence of two small streams on the low ground of Great Meadows, surrounded by forested slopes which furnished excellent protection for any attacking force.

Even the most elementary knowledge of military engineering leads an officer to fortify a high place that is difficult to storm, and to do this, if possible, out of small-arms' range of the nearest natural cover for the opposing troops. Washington evidently reasoned that this open glade was one of the few treeless areas in many miles. Moreover, he knew that his men and horses would need drinking water, not always easily available in these mountains. Using two ravines as natural entrenchments, and boxing the camp with his wagons, Washington flattered himself that he had provided a fairly strong defensive position. He wrote with boyish enthusiasm to Governor Dinwiddie:

> We have, with Nature's assistance, made a good Intrenchment, and by clearing the Bushes out of these Meadows, prepar'd a charming field for an Encounter.

May 25th and 26th were days of tense anticipation at Fort Necessity. New rumors arrived of a French advance probing cautiously through the dark forest. But a strong scouting party failed to find the enemy.

As the shadows began to lengthen over Great Meadows on the evening of the 27th, a storm blew up and rain began to fall. Then into the camp slipped a deeper shadow—an Indian messenger with the appropriate name of Silver-heels. He said that he was bringing a warning from Half King that the footprints of Frenchmen had been seen near by. Half King and a few of his braves were waiting near the craggy retreat where the French were hiding. Washington and some of his men must come at once.

The commander of the fort first placed his ammunition in a safe place with a strong guard to defend it. Then, with an adequate detachment he prepared to follow Silverheels. But let Washington tell the story:

> That very moment I . . . set out in a heavy rain, and in a night as dark as pitch, along a path scarce broad enough for one man; we were sometimes fifteen or twenty minutes out of the path, before we could come to it again, and we would often strike against each other in the darkness: All night long we continued our route, and on the 28th, about sun-rise, we arrived at the Indian Camp, where, after having held a council with the Half King, we concluded to attack them together.

Having thus joined forces with his most dependable Indian ally, George Washington now moved forward to his first military skirmish. Two skillful trackers led the way to the French encampment, and the others followed "Indian fashion" one behind the next. Soon they came upon the "skulking place" where the French were hidden in a secret glen beneath a jutting shelf of rock.

Washington ordered his soldiers and the Indians to spread out in a half-circle to surround this natural stronghold. The French, seeing their danger, ran for their guns and both parties began firing.

Who fired the first shot of the French and Indian War? Was it one of these Frenchmen? Or was it one of Washington's Virginians? Probably we will never know. The French furiously contended that Washington was the responsible party, having attacked an "embassy" which was seeking to bring him a message. But Washington argued that no ambassador comes with a strongly armed force and hides for days to spy upon those to whom he has been sent. Obviously the French, who had already driven the Virginians from the Fork of the Ohio, were here attempting to determine the strength of Washington's army. Conflict between the determined French and the equally determined English would appear to have been inevitable. Washington felt that he was strictly fulfilling his military mission when he attacked this armed French scouting party which had "invaded English soil."

For fifteen minutes there was a lively skirmish. When the French surrendered, ten of their number including their leader, Joseph Coulon de Villiers, Sieur de Jumonville, lay dead upon the ground. Meanwhile one of Washington's men had been killed and two wounded. The Indians immediately scalped the dead Frenchmen and would have scalped the twenty-one prisoners had not Washington intervened. Only one Frenchman escaped, and he fled swiftly through the woods toward Fort Duquesne carrying news that would undoubtedly inspire revenge.

Washington was youthfully exhilarated by this exchange of musketry. He wrote his brother Jack, "I heard the bullets whistle, and, believe me, there is something charming in the sound." Years later, when asked if he had ever made such a remark, Washington answered, "If I said so it was when I was young."

This episode was the famous "assassination" of Jumonville which the French charged to Washington. But their interpretation of the event was not shared by Washington, by Governor Dinwiddie or by the Virginia House of Burgesses, all of whom looked upon this foray as the legitimate repulse of armed intruders.

Among the French captives were two officers whom Washington furnished with clothes from his own scanty wardrobe before ordering them back to Virginia under military escort as prisoners of war. Washington also sent by this escort a message to Dinwiddie requesting that these French gentlemen be treated with due courtesy. He warned the Governor, however, not to be taken in by their "smooth stories."

It was now clear to Washington that he would soon be attacked by a strong French force from Fort Duquesne. And he prepared accordingly.

A long chapter might be written on what transpired between that first exchange of gunfire on May 28th and the battle for Fort Necessity on July 3rd. During that anxious period there were tedious conferences with the Indians, and the exchange of many speeches and wampum belts. But the simple truth was that the Indians were secretly convinced that the Virginians were facing defeat. Not even the arrival of a few English reinforcements changed the fact that Washington and his men were still greatly outnumbered. And to the dusky warriors it was apparent that their white brothers, the English, had chosen an indefensible site for their little fort. Finally all of them, even Half King, deserted and faded away into the silences of the surrounding forest. Sometimes the army was without flour. The men exhausted themselves by cutting a road toward Redstone Creek, then retreated precipitously upon learning of a sizable French expedition sallying forth from

Fort Duquesne. This force was commanded by Captain Louis Coulon de Villiers, brother of the slain Jumonville. And the captain was hungry for revenge.

Fort Necessity had now been improved by the erection of a circular stockade of logs, by the addition of a central storehouse of log construction roofed with deer hides, and also by trenches excavated outside the stockade. But no experienced military eye would have called that swampy meadow "a charming field for an Encounter." Certainly it proved anything but charming on the rainy day of July 3, 1754, when out of the mid-morning mists to the south of the fort an army of French and Indians materialized.

Washington was in command of about 400 soldiers. But of these so many were ill that he had but 184 effective fighting men. To these the enemy opposed perhaps 500 French soldiers plus 400 Indians. Thus the half-starved Virginians were outnumbered by at least three to one. The French appeared in three columns before the fort. The Indians pierced the morning silence with their spine-chilling and ferocious battle cries. Out from the fort sallied the Virginians, as eager for battle as the encroaching enemy.

As Washington moved his once "self-willed, ungovernable" troops onto the rain-soaked, misty meadow, he must have felt a thrill of pride. They formed their unwavering line and stood as though on parade, withholding their fire. At a distance too great for effective musket fire the French came to a halt, raised their guns and fired. No Virginian or Carolinian fell. The English line stood firm, awaiting Washington's command, saving their ammunition for better use at closer range.

When it became apparent that the French and Indians only hoped to lure the English into the woods (where they would have been at great disadvantage), Washington ordered his men into the trenches, which were already filling with water. Now the command was for each man to fire at his discretion.

"From every little rising, tree, stump, stone and bush" the French and Indians began their harassing fire. It was returned with spirit and vigor from the trenches where the muddy water soon was stained with blood.

Then there began what Washington described as the "most tremendous rain" conceivable. Slowly the water rose in the trenches—hip deep, waist deep. But still his men continued to answer the French and Indian fusillade.

The great wonder is that these outnumbered, hungry, weary and half-drowned men of Washington's army, fighting under every imaginable disadvantage, held out as long as they did. All that stormy day the exchange of fire continued. Then, just after dusk, came a cry from the French asking the English to parley.

At first Washington refused, feeling that this was only a ruse by which the French hoped to enter the stockade and scout the predicament of the fort. But the rain continued to fall, and the trenches to flood. In addition to the many sick soldiers lying in the rain, thirty of Washington's men had been killed and seventy more wounded. True, the French were also busy burying their dead, but it was apparent that with their superior numbers they could hold out much longer than those in the flooded fort.

Finally Washington agreed to send two officers, one of whom, Captain Jacob Van Braam supposedly knew French. They were to bring back any written message the French might wish to convey.

Washington's position was indeed hopeless. His powder wet, his food exhausted, his little fort awash and littered with the dead and wounded, he could not have fought another day. Nevertheless he refused one French condition after another during that rainy night, until it finally seemed that he had been offered terms that he could accept with honor.

By sputtering candlelight in the dripping darkness Van Braam haltingly translated from the blotted paper the terms of capitulation.

Nothing this time seemed too greatly amiss. The important points were that the English could return to their homes taking all their baggage and equipment except their few pieces of artillery. They could march out next morning with the honors of war, drum beating. But they must also promise that they would build no "establishment" on the westward side of the mountains for a full year.

Washington paid little attention to the paragraph stating that he had killed Jumonville. Of course his men had killed Jumonville in open battle. But the fatal word in the French tongue was "l'assassinat." Through ignorance or clumsiness Van Braam translated this as "death" or "loss." Washington was obviously responsible for the death or loss of Jumonville. But he would never have signed a document saying he was responsible for his "assassination."

Van Braam had proved before, and he would prove again, that he was a brave and loyal man. It is therefore entirely unlikely that his translation was a piece of trickery. He was doing the best a Dutch soldier could do in that wavering candlelight to translate French into English. However, by an irony of fate, he paid dearly for that error, since he was one of the two hostages given to the French to insure the return of the two French officers previously captured by Washington.

And so that "charming" field of encounter at Great Meadows became a bloody nightmare. Yet the young Colonel believed on the morning of July 4, 1754, that he was retiring with honor from an engagement he could scarcely have won.

He had tasted his first victory and his first defeat. He had learned valuable lessons from both success and failure. In a larger sense he was being tested by fire for a far more important role on an incomparably greater field of action.

He admitted that he had been "soundly beaten," which bespeaks both honesty and good sportsmanship. And he had made a firm resolve to reverse his fortune in the not-too-distant future.

CHAPTER 8

AN AIDE TO BRADDOCK

GEORGE WASHINGTON, LIKE ACHILLES, SULKED IN HIS tent—or rather in his plantation house at Mount Vernon. Governor Dinwiddie had virtually demoted him from colonel to captain by offering him the command of a mere company. Washington rightly considered this to be criticism of his efforts in the late campaign. The young Colonel felt that his *honor* had been slighted.

True, the Virginia House of Burgesses had granted a vote of thanks to Washington and the other officers of the regiment. And he had gracefully replied in letters to the Speaker and the Gentlemen of the House. But Governor

81

Dinwiddie's arbitrary action in breaking Washington's regiment into separate companies, and offering him the command of one of these, was so galling to the proud young Virginian that he had resigned his commission. When Governor Sharpe of Maryland tried to secure his services as an officer for Maryland troops, Washington declined, admitting wistfully, however, that "My inclinations are strongly bent to arms."

Washington had let his private affairs slip into untidy shape while fighting on the frontier. There were many serious problems to occupy his attention on his big Potomac plantation. He also went fishing in the Potomac, donned hunting clothes to chase the fox, and danced with pretty Tidewater girls.

But when rumors began to drift across the Atlantic revealing that both the British and the French were preparing war fleets to bolster their forces in North America, George found it hard to keep his mind on his farming. The British were preparing to meet force with force along the whole wilderness frontier from Nova Scotia through Crown Point and Fort Niagara to Fort Duquesne at the Fork of the Ohio.

General Braddock, a British officer with more than forty

years' service in the Guards, had been chosen to capture Fort Duquesne. When his two regiments of Redcoats with their great train of artillery and other stores and munitions sailed up the Potomac past Mount Vernon under the very eyes of Washington whose inclinations were so "strongly bent to arms" it is not strange that George could think and dream of little else.

Braddock further dramatized the occasion by calling together several colonial governors in a council of war at nearby Alexandria where the major body of troops was encamped. British officers in their scarlet coats were to be seen at every entertainment. The ex-Colonel of the Virginia regiment realized that somehow he must take part in the exciting new campaign to humble the French and recover the Fork of the Ohio.

It is little wonder, therefore, that when he received a letter from Captain Robert Orme, an aide to Braddock, that he broke the seal with haste and rapidly scanned the script:

> *Sir*: The general, having been informed that you expressed some desire to make the campaign ... will be very glad of your company in his family ... I shall think myself very happy to form an acquaintance with a person so universally esteemed ... I am, Sir, your most obedient servant.
>
> ROBERT ORME, *Aide-de-Camp*

Here was an opportunity to serve under the famous Braddock. Actually Washington would be a volunteer officer without rank or pay. However he would also be a member of the General's "family" in the company of such agreeable young gentlemen as Robert Orme, Robert Morris, and William Shirley (son of Governor Shirley of Massachusetts). This was a rare chance to learn the art of war, help whip the hated French, and rise in the opinion of his fellow Virginians. In a letter dated April 20th, 1755, Washington exults in serving "without expectation of reward, or prospect of attaining a Command." He would be a free-lance companion and adviser to the General in his march through the gloomy forests to the Fork of the Ohio.

The relationship between the sixty-year-old Braddock and the twenty-three-year-old Washington was from the first remarkable. In some respects it was that of an indulgent father to an admiring but critical son. It is not surprising that this brave general officer who had made war his profession from earliest youth did not always heed the excellent but sometimes heated advice of a stripling who was the veteran of but one unsuccessful summer campaign.

Washington was impressed by the sheer spectacle of Braddock's seemingly well-trained, smoothly-operating regiments. But he was soon aware that the General had not the slightest notion of the enormous difficulties which would face him on the rugged frontier. The uncommissioned aide-de-camp knew from sorrowful experience, for instance, the extreme difficulty of assembling the needed teams and wagons for dragging stores and munitions over those mountains. From the first he predicted slow progress and long delays. But General Braddock at first made light of all these difficulties, largely because his past experience had not prepared him for the unimaginable struggle ahead.

As an example of Braddock's ridiculous approach to this frontier war, the General set forth from Winchester in the Shenandoah Valley for Fort Cumberland at Wills Creek in a magnificent chariot drawn by six prancing horses, surrounded by his staff and a troop of light horse while drums beat the "Grenadier's March." George Washington, who had already become politely critical, may well have told the plump General that beyond Wills Creek there was scarcely a track through the wilderness, much less a smooth highway to accommodate an elaborate carriage.

Apparently Braddock managed to get his great coach as far as Fort Cumberland where he was properly welcomed with a seventeen-gun salute.

It was pleasant for George to be "freed from all commands but his (Braddock's), and give Orders to all, which must be implicitly obey'd." But it was not so pleasant to find his own dire predictions of interminable delays all too thoroughly justified. It was impossible to move the army forward from Wills Creek without a great train of transport, promised but not delivered by the Virginia, Maryland and Pennsylvania farmers. Had it not been for brilliant Benjamin Franklin, Braddock might have been stalled at Fort Cumberland all summer. Franklin, asking no reward, rounded up and delivered the horses and wagons. He came very near to losing every shilling of his own private fortune in this patriotic venture when the British army delayed payment to the farmers.

The month of May was rapidly passing—a droughty May in contrast to the great rains of the previous year. But whereas mud would be less of a problem to the transport, forage for the horses would be an added difficulty in the dry mountains. Hundreds of wagonloads of feed would need to be transported over those towering hills to feed the laboring teams and the herds of beef cattle driven before the army to furnish fresh meat.

While Braddock was fuming at Wills Creek through the latter half of May, 1755, breathing fire down the necks of the swindling rascals who had promised supplies and transport, Washington was fortunate in being given an exciting and responsible assignment to take his mind off the frustrating delay. He was ordered to return to Williamsburg to bring up a war chest of £4,000 in metal coins. Riding fast, he spared neither himself nor his horses as he dashed down forest trails to the Tidewater, and on to the capital of the colony. When the cash had been assembled, Washington again sprang to the saddle and retraced his route. At Winchester, he was to have been met by a guard of light horse, but none was to be found at the rendezvous. Washington was finally forced to impress a few reluctant militiamen to help guard the treasure through the forests to Wills Creek.

When Washington arrived at the fort with the money, he learned that 500 men under Sir John St. Clair were moving westward to begin clearing a twelve-foot road through the wilderness. Aside from certain detours this was approximately the same route Washington had traversed the previous summer. But for such a large army, with its vastly heavier baggage, a wider, smoother road was needed. Washington had spoken often of the enormous ridges lying ahead. He had early predicted that "our tremendous undertaking of transporting the heavy Artillery over the Mountains . . . will compose the greatest difficulty of the Campaigne . . ."

Today a jet plane can streak from Cumberland, Maryland (Wills Creek) to Pittsburgh (Fort Duquesne) in a matter of flashing minutes. In an automobile, it is a leisurely afternoon drive. But when Braddock's army in that hot, dry June of 1755 was laboring through the tangled woods and underbrush, it was a record day when the overloaded army advanced more than three miles. The mountains rang to the ax-strokes of six hundred woodsmen; the groaning wheels of the covered wagons mingled with the heavy breathing of the overworked men and horses. The army wound like a "slow scarlet worm" through the green forest, eating away at the giant oaks and hickories, maples and beeches, tearing at the wild grapevines as it slashed its way from Wills Creek toward the Fork of the Ohio.

Men and horses suffered from snake bites and from

ticks which burrowed into the skin and drove men screaming mad, causing infections sometimes resulting in amputations and death. Men also died from polluted water, bad food and mysterious fevers. Those who wandered far from camp or lagged behind were likely to stop an arrow or the blade of a tomahawk. At night the wolves howled and every shadow moving through the forest terrified the English soldiers who had never before seen the wilderness and wished never to see it again. It took one month and eight days to move that army 100 miles—an average of about two-and-one-half agonizing miles a day.

Meanwhile, George Washington was becoming increasingly aware of the deficiencies of Braddock, "... who is incapable of Arguing... or giving up any point he asserts, let it be ever so incompatible with Reason."

However, even so stubborn a martinet as Braddock began to see that he could not reach Fort Duquesne before the arrival of the rumored French reinforcements unless he somehow lightened the load of his advance forces. It was George Washington's suggestion that much of the dress clothing and luxurious supplies of the officers be left behind, thus freeing many "bat" horses for better use than this valet service. He also suggested that 1,200 picked men under the General's direct command be sent ahead with the lightest possible equipment. The remainder of the army with the heavy baggage could follow under command of Colonel Dunbar. These suggestions were adopted by Braddock. Nevertheless, the movement of the advance force was intolerably slow.

On other matters equally important Braddock was completely stubborn. He did not realize the need for a screen of Indians and moccasin-footed frontiersmen to comb the forest ahead and on either side of the troops. He loftily waved aside the services of the fabled white woodsman known as Jack the Black Hunter (or Black Rifle). This "terror of the Indians" and his trusted men needed "no shelter for the night" and asked no pay. They roamed the forests like panthers or owls, and could play the Indian game better than the savages themselves. But proud, pompous Braddock was certain he needed no such scouts and guides. He would have reason to regret his stupid self-assurance.

Blundering slowly and noisily through the forest toward the Monongahela, his movements were about as secret and silent as those of a herd of buffalo. And although it has been recorded that the French were mortally afraid of this great army moving toward them, there was never the slightest doubt at Fort Duquesne as to the number, whereabouts, and progress per day of Braddock's forces.

It was at just this time, when Braddock most needed Washington's constant advice, that George fell dangerously ill. Despite his violent protests, he was left behind to travel with Colonel Dunbar's lagging troops, far in the rear of the spearhead of the column seeking battle. Writing to his brother Jack, whom he had left in charge of Mount Vernon, he explained that it had been Braddock's absolute orders that he travel with Dunbar's regiment. But Washington had made the General promise that he would be called forward in time to join in the battle for the fort. To his fellow aide-de-camp, Robert Orme, he sent the following message:

> *Dear Orme:*
> My Fevers are very moderate, and I hope are near a Crisis; when I shall have nothing to encounter but excessive weakness, and the difficulty of getting to you; which I would not fail in doing ere you reach Duquisne, for £500, but I have no doubt of doing this, as the General has given me his word and honour, in the most solemn manner ..."

Braddock, who was genuinely fond of young Washington, was as good as his word. In a memorandum in his letter book George tells how he hurried forward to be present at the battle, sick and miserable though he was.

> The 8th of July I rejoined (in a covered Waggon) the advanced division of the Army under the immediate Com'd of the General. On the 9th I attended him on horse back tho' very weak and low . . .

That historic 9th of July was the great and fatal day. Most of the officers who arose that morning would not see the sunset, nor would hundreds of their men. George Washington, so wan and ill that he was propped into his saddle with a pillow, had never been more happy as he watched that apparently grave, perfectly disciplined army begin its last few miles toward the French fort. The rising sun shone upon a sight to thrill any young man whose inclinations were "strongly bent to arms." Stepping forward to brisk commands in perfect formation went Braddock's army. How could skulking savages and a few Frenchmen face such a fighting force? Ambuscades? Nonsense. Braddock's Redcoats would soon eliminate any such petty annoyance.

Washington, in remembering this scene of scarlet coats and gleaming muskets, was to describe it as "the most beautiful spectacle I ever beheld."

Because it was impossible at this point to follow the steep and craggy north bank of the Monongahela directly to Fort Duquesne, Braddock had ordered the army to ford the stream, to descend the easy south bank for six miles, and then to re-ford the river just below the mouth of Turtle Creek. The first crossing was accomplished without incident, and the troops made relatively swiftprogress to the second crossing.

This second fording of the river, taking place as it did at high noon on a bright summer day, was a remarkable sight in this remote wilderness. Colors flying and uniforms blazing, the horses and men splashed through the clear water to the northern shore. The artillery, consisting of 12-pounders, howitzers and mortars, glistened in the shallow stream. White-covered wagons contrasted with the blue of sky and water.

Amazingly no French or Indians were present at this strategic spot to dispute their passage. Officers and men, forgetting their painful struggle through the mountains, were radiant with happiness. In a matter of hours, they had reason to believe they would be lining up before the terrified fort and demanding its surrender. Then the whole valley of the Ohio would have fallen to the British almost without a shot and the French would be ousted forever. On the north shore of the Monongahela, Braddock halted the entire column to arrange the final order of march. Then the officers pinned their white napkins around their necks (as was proper in those days) and prepared to eat a leisurely noon meal.

Meanwhile, at the nearby Fork of the Ohio, the commander, Contrecoeur, had been considering the advisability of abandoning the newly completed French fort. Vastly outnumbered by the British, and not too certain of the loyalty of the Ojibwas, Hurons, Ottawas, Delawares and other miscellaneous Indian tribes living in bark huts around the fort, he felt that his chances of winning a pitched battle with Braddock were slight indeed.

However, a certain Captain Beaujeu pleaded with his senior officer to be allowed to sally forth with an attacking party of French, Canadians and Indians and to harry the approaching British regiments. Beaujeu was a brave young man and a determined one. However, his first two appeals to the Indians were met with sullen refusal. Not even the bravest of these forest warriors wished to be sacrificed to the many muskets and heavy artillery they had seen moving through the mountains. Finally Beaujeu threw down his tomahawk and cried to the savages, "I am determined to go out and meet the enemy . . . Will you suffer your father to go out alone?"

This challenge seemed to shame the Indians. One band after another agreed to accompany the French officer.

On the morning of July 9th, while the Redcoats were moving with blithe assurance down the Monongahela toward the second crossing, the Indians were singing and dancing and working themselves into a pitch of fighting frenzy outside Fort Duquesne. Kegs of powder and shot were broken open by the French, and the savages were invited to help themselves.

By this time Beaujeu had been joined by two other captains, four lieutenants, six ensigns and two cadets. These officers plus seventy-two French regulars, 146 youthful Canadians and perhaps 700 Indians made a total of slightly more than 900 fighting men, most of them crafty and experienced in the ways of forest encounter. They were setting forth to meet some 1,500 soldiers under the self-assured Braddock.

It had been Beaujeu's intention to ambush the British at the second ford. However, due to the delay caused by the dancing Indians, the French war party was slow in getting started. To Beaujeu's consternation the British were already safely across the Monongahela and had extended their line of march a full mile toward the Fort when he and his Indians discovered them. Beaujeu, far from ambushing the British, came upon them unexpectedly, blundering head on into their scouts, engineers and a small body of light horse. There was a French volley, scattered fire, and then a volley in reply from the British. Beaujeu, thinking swiftly, waved half his line to the right of the British column and half to the left. Then he himself advanced bravely toward their center, his silver gorget shining on his breast. A British bullet found its mark and for him the sky darkened. He could not know that his quick wit and gallantry had already won the day for France.

The astonished English troops were also taken by surprise. The scattering of scouts, pioneers, engineers, light horse and grenadiers, meeting unsuspected opposition, began to fall back on the advance guard. Huddled like cattle in their twelve-foot lane through the forest, these frightened soldiers could see nothing of the enemy save the puffs of blue smoke or the dark gleam of an occasional bronze warrior dashing momentarily from cover to scalp a victim before disappearing, as though by magic, into the dense greenery.

The English were paying dearly at this point for their lack of Indian and frontier scouts, their ignorance of frontier warfare, and their complete unfamiliarity with the terrain. But the French, who for all their woodcraft had also been surprised, were in blind luck in stumbling upon this excellent site for annihilating the British. The battleground, which is now within the Borough of Braddock in metropolitan Pittsburgh, was at that time lush forest. The road being cut by Braddock's axmen ran, by ill fortune, between two ravines which gave perfect cover to the French and Indians. From these natural trenches they could pour from both sides a murderous fire into the helpless British and Virginia troops.

When they heard the sound of guns, the British officers who were still eating their leisurely meal on the banks of the Monongahela mounted their horses and galloped to the scene of action, some of them still wearing their white napkins at their necks. No braver group of men ever tried to rally a crazed army. Tall, crimson-coated, and riding their frightened horses up and down that 12-foot alley of death between the trees, they fell one after another. Sixty-three of the eighty-six commissioned officers were soon killed or wounded.

Attacked in front and on both sides by an enemy they could not see, the men themselves were near to hysteria. In their brilliant red coats they were as obvious as scarlet tanagers in a willow tree, perfect targets for the French and their savage allies. There was the maddening, dismaying fact that most of the men in that bloody mile still had not seen a single enemy. And yet the bullets from invisible muskets whistled into their withering ranks with a hail of death. Huddling together and driven as "Sheep before Hounds" (to use Washington's colorful phrase) they loaded and fired completely at random, killing more of their own men than of the enemy. Once when a contingent of buckskin-clad Virginians tried to move through the trees to capture a ravine, the Redcoats, seeing a target for the first time, annihilated almost the entire company.

As both Washington and Orme were later to testify,

the officers fought and died magnificently. Braddock had five horses shot from under him before he himself was shot through the shoulder and lung, a wound which would soon prove fatal. Washington, barely up from his sickbed, carried Braddock's orders through that storm of musket balls, organizing resistance wherever he could. He pleaded to be allowed to lead a charge up the hill to clear one of the ravines, but Braddock shook his head. Two horses were shot from under Washington. Bullets pierced his hat. Four times they ripped his clothes. But still this determined young man fought on.

When all was lost—when most of the Virginians and most of the officers had been killed, when the wagoners had cut loose their horses and fled, when 714 of Braddock's soldiers had been killed or wounded—Washington managed to move the mortally wounded Braddock across the Monongahela. Of the General's "family," Orme and Morris were badly wounded and Shirley was dead. But George Washington emerged without a scratch.

Fortunately the savages did not follow the British retreat across the Monongahela. In accordance with their bloody custom, they remained on the field of battle to scalp the dead and wounded and to collect the loot.

Meanwhile the panic-stricken British army continued to retreat as though fiends were following them. They fell back upon Colonel Dunbar, who instead of rallying and reinforcing them became himself so panicked that he burned his baggage, attempted to destroy his artillery, and began his flight back toward Fort Cumberland.

Washington, who had been helped into his saddle at dawn on the morning of the 9th, remained astride one horse or another for more than twenty-four hours, having fought with unwavering bravery and having carried his wounded chief from the field. He tenderly moved Braddock far back along the tortuous trail where that courageous but mistaken officer was soon to die.

To his brother at Mount Vernon, George wrote from Fort Cumberland:

> *Dear Jack:* As I have heard since my arriv'l at this place, a circumstantial acct. of my death and dying speech, I take this early opportunity of contradicting both, and of assuring you that I now exist and appear in the land of the living by the miraculous care of Providence, that protected me beyond all human expectation...
>
> We have been most scandalously beaten by a trifling body of men; but fatigue and want of time prevents me from giving any of the details...

Washington then believed that the enemy numbered no more than 300 (about one-third the actual force of French and Indians). He was thus one of the few officers in history who ever was so modest as to underestimate the strength of an army by which he was beaten. In another respect, too, he showed his modesty. He did not take to himself credit for his bravery and his excellent advice to Braddock. Nor did he spare praise to others who fought with courage. However he knew stupidity and cowardice when he saw them.

To Governor Dinwiddie he wrote:

> The officers in gen'l behav'd with incomparable bravery, for which they greatly suffer'd. . . . The Virginian Companies behav'd like Men and died like Soldiers; for I believe out of the 3 Companys that were there that day, scarce 30 were left alive: . . . In short the dastardly behavior of the English Soldiers expos'd all those who were inclin'd to do their duty to almost certain Death; and at length, in despight of every effort to the contrary, broke and ran as Sheep before Hounds . . . and when we endeavour'd to rally them in hopes of regaining our invaluable loss, it was with as much success as if we had attempted to have stop'd the wild Bears of the Mountains. The Genl. was wounded behind in the shoulder, and into the Breast, of w'ch he died three days after.

In almost his final words, Braddock is reported to have said with a deep sigh, "We shall know better another time."

In more than one respect, however, Braddock and his masters in London were learning too late. Already there were many in the American colonies whose respect for the Redcoats was on the wane, and whose admiration for Washington and the colonial troops was, on the contrary, blossoming toward patriotic loyalty and fervor. As Benjamin Franklin recorded in his *Autobiography*, "This whole transaction gave us the first suspicion that our exalted ideas of the prowess of British regular troops had not been well founded." Thus one of many new ideas had been implanted which would finally explode in the American Revolution.

Reverend Samuel Davies (later President of Princeton University) used Washington as the subject of a sermon at about this time. He called him "a remarkable instance" of patriotic spirit and military ardor, and hoped that this "heroic youth" had been preserved by Providence "for some important service to his country."

CHAPTER 9

FRONTIER AND
METROPOLIS

THROUGHOUT HIS LIFE WASHINGTON JUSTIFIED HIS reputation for overcoming difficulties, enduring privations and reversing defeats. However, he was at no time a brainless optimist. Like most other human beings he had his moments of despair.

One such moment was in the mid-summer of 1755 after his return to Mount Vernon following the disaster on the Monongahela. Washington was young. He was ill. And he felt such personal responsibility for the misfortune of Braddock's army that he called it "our shameful defeat . . . so scandalous that I hate to have it mention'd."

In his three excursions into the wilderness, Washington's intentions had been excellent, his actions brave and his luck very poor. In a letter to his half-brother Augustine, dated August 2, 1755, he summed up his misfortunes on those three occasions to show that he had been "upon the losing order" ever since he had entered the service.

However, no one knew better than Washington the danger to the entire frontier since Braddock's defeat and Dunbar's "monstrous" retreat with 1,500 soldiers from Fort Cumberland to Philadelphia, where he had gone into "winter quarters" in August.

There was a public clamor asking that Washington command an "enlarged regiment" for which the House of Burgesses had voted funds. And although Washington was reluctant to accept a commission to lead a regiment which so far existed only on paper, he finally accepted the command.

The proposed force of 4,000 Virginians swiftly dwindled to a possible 1,200 of whom scarcely a full company was anywhere available for action. Despite his long illness, Washington from early September was busy inspecting Virginia's defenses. He discovered an almost incredible state of unpreparedness.

At Williamsburg he found that the arsenal had been

stripped of munitions by Dinwiddie to help the northern colonists in other campaigns against the French. In Fredericksburg where half-naked ne'er-do-wells had been drafted, it was necessary to keep them in the local jail to prevent them from deserting. In Alexandria the few troops available were mostly barefooted. And at Winchester in the Shenandoah Valley, any call for the militia was a bitter joke; no one responded. At Fort Cumberland, just across the line in Maryland, there were less than 100 effective fighting men. In short, the rampaging French and Indians had little to fear along the whole unprotected frontier.

The young commander in chief had reason to worry. His problems of supply seemed almost beyond repair. What few men he had were virtually without clothes (and to be barefooted, as Washington himself admitted, was a valid excuse for refusing to march or fight). There was a shortage of all kinds of food—corn, beef, and even flour. Washington engaged coopers to make barrels for the pickling of beef. He haggled with profiteers who were trying to cheat the army. He tried to regulate the disastrously heavy sale of liquor to the troops, a headache in many wars before and since.

Transportation, a major problem in the two recent

campaigns, now became an all-but-impossible bottleneck. Virginia had not repaid the desperate farmers for horses and wagons impressed by Braddock. Now nothing less than a threat of force could produce a wagon or team.

Discipline was practically nonexistent. The severe articles of war, with death penalties for certain grave offenses, had lapsed with the defeat of Braddock. Desertions were constant; mutiny was frequent. Washington pleaded with Williamsburg for new regulations to help him discipline the lazy and drunken troops and unconcerned officers.

Add the utter irresponsibility of the commissary, the weird bookkeeping of the paymasters, the demand of the officers for bounties to be paid for recruits who never appeared, the embezzlement of supplies by ships' captains on the Potomac, the shoddy quality of clothing delivered to the army, the skin-and-bones condition of the cattle sent from the Carolinas and the lack of all munitions of war—and you can easily see why Washington was sometimes on the verge of despair. Except for a very few responsible fellow officers, he was almost the only Virginian in the new "regiment" interested in defending the exposed frontier.

But one of Washington's best characteristics was his ability to shake off his despondency and rise to his responsibilities in time of crisis. Early in October he was galvanized into action by the report that the French and Indians had swept down upon the frontier, burning and scalping. Colonel Washington, who had been hastening toward Williamsburg on military business, wheeled his horse and galloped back toward the menaced and flaming frontier.

The whole Shenandoah Valley was in a state of utmost panic. So many cavalcades of terrified settlers were streaming back through the gaps in the Blue Ridge that it was all but impossible to use the trails for reinforcements of militia moving toward the valley. The frontiersmen believed that the French and Indians were on their very heels and that Winchester was in flames.

The town was not in flames, Washington discovered, but it was in the utmost confusion. There seemed to be no reliable knowledge as to the whereabouts and strength of the enemy. Washington dispatched scouts to scour the woods for intelligence. He sent orders to the officers of small outlying forts commanding them to resist to the utmost. Then he attempted to raise the local militia but found that scarcely a man would stir, "...choosing as they say to die, with their Wives and Familys."

One can sympathize with these endangered frontier people in their outlying cabins, utterly defenseless against tomahawk and flaming arrow, particularly if the men of the family want off with the militia. But one can also sympathize with Washington, trying vainly to assemble a few fighting men for the general defense of the whole frontier.

Almost the only cool head in that panic-stricken valley was the 23-year-old Commander. He put smiths to work repairing arms, and impressed what few horses and wagons he could obtain, sending them for flour, musket balls, flints and powder. More scouts and spies were sent to reconnoiter. And messages were expressed by galloping courier to the Tidewater to hurry recruits from below.

In all these things Washington met with "the greatest opposition." No orders were obeyed "but what a Party of Soldiers, or my own drawn Sword, Enforces..." In fact the terrified inhabitants threatened "to blow out my Brains." Nevertheless the young Colonel in the next sentence speaks of "the poor distressed People, who were drove from their Habitations." Despite their obstinacy and panic, he was doing everything within his limited power for them.

There was no doubt that the French and Indians had attacked the frontier and had murdered, scalped and burned. However their number appears to have been grossly exaggerated. The alarms which messengers "spent with fatigue and fear" brought to Washington were heightened by vivid imagination, easily stimulated under such spine-chilling conditions.

When on a Sunday morning there arrived a frantic message, "... ten times more terrified ... with information that the Indians had got within four Miles of the Town, and were killing and destroying all before them . . ." Washington prepared to sally forth to meet the enemy. For had not the messenger himself heard "constant Firing, and the Shrieks of the unhappy Murder'd?"

Upon receiving this literally hair-raising report, Washington "... immediately collected what Force" he could, a pitiful little company consisting of twenty-two rangers and nineteen militiamen under the personal command of the Colonel. In Washington's words, they marched "directly to the place where these horrid Murders were said to be committed. When we came

there, whom should we find occasioning all this distur-
bance, but 3 drunken Soldiers of the Light-Horse, carous-
ing, firing their pistols, and uttering the most unheard of
Imprecations."

A ludicrous story, and Washington seems to have
relished its irony. But how much it tells of his bravery!

In this same message to the Governor, Washington
reveals that his scouts, coming in next morning, informed
him that the Indians, who had been about 150 in number,
had apparently now left the country. "Seventy or near it of
our People are kill'd and missing." And several houses and
plantations had been destroyed; "but not so great havock
made as was at first represented."

Nevertheless, that second week of October, 1755, had not
been a pleasant one in which to enjoy the flaming autumn
colors of the Shenandoah. And not all of the crimson
splashes on the ground were fallen maple leaves.

After the Indian scare had subsided, Washington continued with his wearying problem of raising and training
reluctant recruits, obtaining supplies from slothful com-
missaries, building small forts along the branches of the
Potomac and cutting a new and better road to Fort
Cumberland. He was still facing major problems of deser-

tions, drunkenness, looting, cowardice and numerous other offenses, and he continued to press the Governor for regulations sufficiently severe so that he could control his troops.

To add to his difficulties, an insolent independent captain named John Dagworthy, in command of a mere thirty Marylanders at Fort Cumberland, not only refused to take orders from the commander of this section of the frontier, but insisted that he himself was in command of the entire fort. Washington had assigned Lieutenant Colonel Adam Stephen to Fort Cumberland, but Dagworthy would not recognize Stephen's senior rank. Such insubordination on the part of the captain was not only embarrassing, it created a situation which was downright dangerous to the defense of the whole area.

Washington has been criticized for making such a large issue of Dagworthy's little rebellion. And indeed there is a ridiculous aspect to the affair, with the young Colonel seeming to behave in a rather pompous and stiff-necked manner, making too much of a point of "honor." However, the situation had serious implications both then and later. This same thorny problem which Washington had first faced when Captain Mackay had refused to take orders at Fort Necessity was subtly weakening the entire English cause.

The haughty contention that any commission in His Majesty's regular military establishment outranked even the highest commissions in the Colonial forces was galling and infuriating to brave officers in every colony. Fort Cumberland was in a constant ferment, with officer factions growing increasingly bitter. In the case of another French and Indian attack, such internal dissension might cost the British dearly. Obviously something must be done to determine once and for all whether a Maryland captain who once held a Royal Commission could refuse to take orders from the Commander of the western frontier.

There was only one officer in the colonies who had sufficient power to settle this vexing problem, and that was Governor Shirley of Massachusetts. He was also at this time commander in chief of all the British military forces in North America. Therefore when Washington asked Governor Dinwiddie if he might take leave of absence to ride in person to Boston, to lay the matter before Shirley, Dinwiddie gave his willing consent.

• • •

Washington's winter journey to warn the French in 1753–1754 had been arduous, dangerous and lonely. His winter journey two years later was pleasant, without danger and highly social. He was now preparing to make a round trip of almost one thousand miles with delightful interludes in Philadelphia, New York City and Boston and with a personal retinue worthy of an officer and a gentleman.

True, the roads were but a slight improvement upon the trails through the wilderness; and many of the wayside inns left much to be desired. But Washington looked forward with keen anticipation to the whole experience.

The Virginia colonel could don buckskins and moccasins when necessary, and sleep beneath the open sky. But on this occasion and on many others in later life he dressed and lived in the luxurious manner of his class.

He was accompanied on this trip by two captains of the Virginia regiment and two liveried body servants. His fellow officers, who must have looked upon this journey as something of a lark, were his aide-de-camp Captain George Mercer and Captain Robert Stewart. George's servants, Thomas Bishop and another, completed the party of five well-mounted men who set forth from Alexandria early in February, 1756.

They must have made a vivid picture against the snowy background of that February morning. If the two captains were dressed in the manner suggested by Washington in a memorandum to all his officers, they wore ". . . an uniform Dress . . . of fine Broad Cloath; The Coat Blue, faced and cuffed with Scarlet, and Trimmed with Silver; The Waistcoat Scarlet, with a plain Silver Lace . . . the Breeches . . . Blue; . . . with a Silver-laced Hat, of a Fashionable size."

The two body servants were, if possible, even more flamboyantly arrayed. Colonel Washington had but recently ordered their livery of cream-colored cloth with "trimmings and facings of scarlet, and a scarlet waistcoat." All this was trimmed with lace, and each had a silver-laced hat. Their coats bore Washington's coat of arms in snowy white.

The colonel himself, we may be sure, had the handsomest clothes of the entire cavalcade. We know that he had recently purchased "1 fashionable gold-laced hat," and that he had "gold and scarlet" sword knots and "silver and blue" of the same. The cloaks to protect all this elegance matched the uniforms. And although the finest of these dress uniforms doubtless had been safely packed for use on social occasions, even the riding clothes of this fashionable party must have been colorful.

We can see them on that frosty morning, their horses prancing and blowing steam from their nostrils. Wheeling northward with a final wave to their friends, these five set off by way of Annapolis, New Castle and Brandywine Ferry. When, after several chilly days, they reached the neat and prosperous metropolis of Philadelphia, they were well rewarded. This 18th-century town with its paved streets and 3,000 or more houses was then the largest city in America. We may be sure that the entertainment offered by prominent citizens was worthy of the already famous young Virginia Colonel.

In New York, Washington was the guest of Beverley Robinson (son of Washington's friend, John Robinson, Speaker of the Virginia House of Burgesses). This former Virginian had settled in New York City and was happily and profitably married to Susannah Philipse, older sister of the equally attractive Mary ("Polly") Philipse. These wealthy co-heiresses of the vast acreage of Philipse Manor were gracious and charming toward the Virginia officers passing through their city.

In partial repayment for their warm hospitality, Washington took the Philipse sisters to an entertaining display which was then the talk of the town. This widely heralded exhibition was called "The Microcosm, or World in Miniature."

Washington himself was of an inventive turn of mind. It must have delighted the colonel as much as it did the heiresses to see an entire little world filled with mechanical miniatures, all in perfect proportion and magically animated. Here was a Roman temple with the nine muses playing a concert on tiny musical instruments ... Orpheus plucking his lyre . . . ships sailing . . . coaches pulled by Lilliputian horses . . . men sawing wood. It was, in fact, a fairy-tale wonderland "all moving easily and gracefully."

Easily and gracefully too moved the young women, noted for their charm as well as for their wealth. It has been said that George Washington proposed to "Polly" Philipse and was refused. However, there is no real evidence that he laid his heart at her feet to have it gently spurned. But there is proof in his account book that he twice visited that small dream world of little figures— a place where a young Virginia officer and a pretty girl could view a land of make-believe.

The trip to Boston was in bitter weather. But during his several days in that northern capital, Washington achieved at least one of his ardent desires. He did not, it is true, manage to acquire for himself and his officers royal commissions in the British Army. (In fact, he would never have that satisfaction.) But he did induce Governor Shirley to settle the Dagworthy dilemma. The Governor wrote out for Washington the following memo:

> *Boston, 5 March, 1756*
> Governor Dinwiddie, at the instance of Colonel Washington, having referred to me concerning the right of command between him and Captain Dagworthy, and desiring that I should determine it, I do therefore give it as my opinion, that Captain Dagworthy, who now acts under a commission from the Governor of Maryland, can only take rank as a provincial Captain and of course is under the command of all field officers and, in case it should happen, that Colonel Washington and Captain Dagworthy should join at Fort Cumberland, it is my order that Colonel Washington shall take the command.
> W. SHIRLEY

Sweet are the fruits of even such a minor victory! But not as sweet as Washington at first imagined. It would be some days before he learned that his success in this matter was far from complete. Although Dagworthy had been quietly reprimanded in this memorandum, Governor Sharpe, the motivating force behind that upstart Maryland captain, had been appointed by Shirley as the officer in supreme command of all the troops in South Carolina, Virginia, Maryland and Pennsylvania for the coming year's action on the frontier. The best Washington could hope for was a position as second in command under an officer he distrusted and disliked.

As Washington and his cavalcade rode back over the muddy and icy roads toward Virginia, he contemplated the advisability of resigning his commission. However the worsening situation on the frontier drove from his mind any such course of action. The Indians and French were again terrifying the entire Shenandoah Valley. And Washington as usual rose to the occasion.

After reporting to Governor Dinwiddie in Williamsburg, George rode posthaste to Winchester where the frontier families were again fleeing the valley.

The leaves of the forest were a delicate green; the fruit trees and the dogwood were in bloom. But against this backdrop of beauty, what misery! No food! No ammunition! No more than forty armed men available for the defense of Winchester. Washington would again do everything within his power. But after an almost futile two weeks trying to organize the defense of the town he wrote to Governor Dinwiddie:

> I am too little acquainted, Sir, with pathetic language, to attempt a description of the people's distresses . . . the murder of poor innocent babes and helpless families . . . The Supplicating tears of the women, and moving petitions from the men, melt me to such deadly sorrow, that I solemnly declare . . . I could offer myself a willing sacrifice to the butchering enemy, provided that would contribute to the people's ease"

Twenty-four-year-old Colonel Washington, in a frontier town with less than half a company of half-armed men, prepared to face the enemy. Already he had become the single pillar of strength to whom a frightened people instinctively turned for their protection.

CHAPTER 10

FORTUNES OF WAR
AND OF LOVE

IN TIME THE INDIANS AND FRENCH DRIFTED BACK to the Ohio. It was clearly apparent, however, that they could repeat their demoralizing raids almost at will. From the first, Washington wisely insisted that the best defense is the offense. He believed that the only way to correct this intolerable situation was to send a strong force to capture Fort Duquesne.

During the years 1756 and 1757 Washington's advice was seldom heeded. Governor Dinwiddie and his friends in Williamsburg were defense-minded. They were stubbornly determined to build a long chain of little forts from the Potomac south to the border of North Carolina. By the wandering trails of those days, this was a meandering "front" of almost 350 miles. Since Washington seldom had more than 700 men under his direct command, he had at the most two men to the mile to defend that frontier. Grouping his soldiers in platoons or undermanned companies in tiny forts appeared to be inviting disaster. None of these toy stockades could resist a serious attack. Moreover the Indians could slip through this coarse screen of defense like water through a sieve.

Washington argued that the forts would be expensive to build and maintain and almost impossible to supply and man. Besides, they would hopelessly scatter his small fighting force. His counter-proposal was to erect one really strong fort and central military base at Winchester.

As a compromise, both the big fort and the little ones were eventually built. The large one at Winchester was called Fort Loudoun in honor of the Earl of Loudoun. It was he who in July, 1756, arrived in America to command all British and colonial forces in the war against the French.

Loudoun soon proved as ineffective as either Braddock

or Shirley before him. Faced by the brilliant new French commander, the Marquis de Montcalm, he was consistently outwitted and outmaneuvered in the north. Benjamin Franklin compared this dilatory general to St. George on the tavern signs—always on horseback but never getting anywhere. His glacial slowness in 1756 and 1757 created an air of depression everywhere, especially among the soldiers stationed on the inactive Virginia-Maryland-Pennsylvania frontier. Washington struggled valiantly but often vainly against the headaches and heartaches of his restless regiment.

To add to his woes, the Virginia commander in the late summer of 1757 was stricken by increasingly severe attacks of dysentery—an illness of which many brave men died in those days. A short rest at Mount Vernon in August helped him to regain some of his strength. But a new attack early in November rendered him unfit for command. Today we know that continued worry and frustration can make a person physically ill. Two years of waiting in vain for a new westward drive against Fort Duquesne may have contributed much to Washington's misery.

By the 9th of November the twenty-five-year-old colonel was in such helpless condition that he was ordered home to his plantation to recover. In the month of January, 1758, he was wishing he might make a trip to Williamsburg, but was still too ill for such a journey.

To Colonel Stanwix he wrote:

> My constitution is certainly greatly impaired. . . . I now have no prospect left of preferment in the military way, and as I despair of rendering that immediate service, which my country may require . . . I have some thoughts of quitting my command . . . leaving my post to be filled by some other person more capable of the task, and who may, perhaps, have his endeavors crowned with better success than mine have been.

Washington has often been pictured as the flawless and almost superhuman Father of his Country—an austere man both saintly and wooden who faced every disaster unflinchingly. He was a brave man, no doubt about it, but much braver than such a false image would indicate. Like all mankind he knew hours of bleak discouragement. Often he felt that his "honor" had been dimmed, but he was eager to burnish it bright once again by further public service. He suffered from moments of depression, but he rose above them. He was a greater man for having had his periods of doubt.

Slowly now he began to regain his health and with it his hope. Although this new year of 1758 would bring additional dark moments, it also held in store at least three victories for Washington: one in love, one in politics, and one in war.

The first was his victory in love. It will be remembered that George had been singularly unsuccessful with the Virginia beauties he had known, even when he had attempted to woo them with passionate poetry. Back in New York City his friend Roger Morris had won the hand of wealthy "Polly" Philipse. In Washington's case, Cupid's archery had so far consistently missed the target.

Now on a trip to Williamsburg he met a rich and pretty widow named Martha Dandridge Custis. She had two handsome children, 150 slaves and 17,000 fertile acres. She has been described as a slightly plump, comfortable and sensible little body with hazel eyes, light brown hair, and feet which took shoes of the "smallest fives." She was deft with her needle and could play the spinet.

How and where they first met is a matter of conjecture. The date has been placed variously in 1758 from March to June, although it might well have been earlier. Virginia was a cozy little community where everyone of wealth knew everyone else. There is, therefore, the distinct possibility that George and Martha had known each other casually for years. Perhaps Washington visited her at Six Chimney House, the Custis residence in Williamsburg. Or perhaps he paid a social call at her plantation on the York River.

In late May Washington was in Williamsburg on military business. He was not a man who usually lingered when on a mission of duty. But tradition says that his servant Bishop waited for hours with the horses while Washington talked with the attractive little widow.

Martha's first husband, Daniel Parke Custis, had died during the previous year, leaving to his 26-year-old wife, and to his small son John and his little daughter Martha a total estate of about $100,000.

The widow Custis needed a husband, a foster father for her two children, and as she frankly admitted, a manager for her estate. How could she do better than by accepting this tall, courtly and already famous Virginia Colonel, who obviously fulfilled all the specifications?

Washington, similarly, needed a wife, a mistress for Mount Vernon, and a pleasant and affectionate companion. Martha was pretty, wealthy and willing. Perhaps they were also in love. Certainly they were to live a contented life together.

Back in Winchester, Washington was soon ordering "by the first ship bound to any part of Virginia . . . as much of the best superfine blue cotton velvet as will make a coat, waist-coat and breeches for a tall man, with a fine silk button to suit it . . . six pairs of the very neatest shoes . . . (and) six pair gloves . . ."

Meanwhile Martha was preparing an invoice which included "One genteel suite of clothes for myself to be grave but not extravagant," plus several feminine items of more intimate apparel.

Obviously there was a fashionable wedding in the offing as soon as Washington could drive the French from Fort Duquesne, and honorably return from the war.

Washington's second victory that year was in politics. While stationed at Fort Cumberland, awaiting further orders, he remembered that a Virginia election was approaching. Washington made no political speeches. He refused to leave his regiment even long enough for a brief appearance in Winchester, from which county seat he hoped to be elected to the Virginia House of Burgesses.

Nevertheless he won the election by a comfortable margin and gladly footed a large tavern bill for food and refreshments for all.

A man who served as "Washington's proxy" in Winchester on that happy day was carried through the streets, while the citizens loudly offered "General applause and Huzzaing for Colonel Washington," the new Burgess from Frederick County.

The third victory was a relatively easy military one. After tedious delays, and a bitter controversy over which route to take through the Pennsylvania wilderness, Washington reluctantly accepted the decision of the British high command.

Ignoring Washington's advice, the British insisted upon cutting a new road rather than using the trail which he and Braddock had slashed so painfully through the mountains farther to the south. When every argument Washington could muster had failed to move Brigadier General John Forbes and Colonel Henry Bouquet, Washington, like the good soldier he always was, led his troops by the northern route that went through Raystown (now Bedford) in the vicinity of the present Pennsylvania Turnpike.

Needless to say there was no smooth four-lane cement highway in those days with easy grades. Nor were there comfortable tunnels through ridges neatly labeled Blue Mountain, Kittatinny Mountain, Tuscarora Mountain, Sideling Hill, Rays Hill, Allegheny Mountain and Laurel Hill. The only way over these man-killing mountains, ranging upward to more than 6,000 feet, was by manpower, horsepower and sheer willpower. Once again Washington's men must labor to build a new road as the season grew later and more chill. Now frost painted the hills with the pale gold of the beeches, the leather-brown of the oaks and the scarlet of sumac and maples.

There was little time for appreciation of this beauty, however, as the hungry and poorly clothed man shivered in the raw winds of autumn. Soon November skies released cascades of icy rain. Would they reach Fort Duquesne before snow made the mountains impassable, and before the brief enlistments ran out?

Washington's men were keyed for battle and for revenge. An advance party had been bloodily repulsed. It was something of an anti-climax, therefore, to stand before the smoking ruins of Fort Duquesne on November 25th, 1758, and to realize that the French had blown up their fort and fled. But now the British flag could fly at the Fork of the Ohio. Soon there would rise upon this site Fort Pitt, named for the vigorous new Prime Minister, William Pitt, whose policies were saving an empire for England. And here in the promising future would one day stand Pittsburgh, the mighty city of smoke and steel.

It was pleasant to have won a campaign at last; pleasant to be lauded in an affectionate farewell written by his officers. Tired and ill, but also happy and hopeful, the young Colonel was now free to return to Virginia, to his bride-to-be, and to his peaceful plantation house at Mount Vernon above the slow-flowing "River of Swans."

That year and the next spelled disaster for the French and success for the British. The two great powers had been struggling for the North American continent for seventy years. They had fought four wilderness wars for the great prize: King William's War; Queen Anne's War; King George's War' and now the last and costliest of the series, the French and Indian War. In the coming year General Wolfe would make his brave attack up the goat path to the Plains of Abraham before Quebec. Both he and the equally gallant Montcalm would fall in that battle, which would seal forever the fate of the French upon this continent.

Cast out of the Eden they had found in North America—the shining St. Lawrence, the Great Lakes, the Belle Rivière that the English called the Ohio—the French and their power from now on would be merely a haunting memory.

On the Gaspé Peninsula and in Quebec, French customs would survive. Far in the remote forest would still be heard the *chansons* of the *coureurs de bois* and the swift lilt of the French tongue. But the flag of France would no longer fly above the missions and trading posts and villages of an island empire. North America would never now become a French-speaking continent. Wolfe and Montcalm had fallen. Quebec had surrendered. And history had been altered for generations yet unborn.

A FASHIONABLE
WEDDING

ON JANUARY 6, 1759, GEORGE WASHINGTON WAS married to Martha Dandridge Custis in her comfortable plantation house on the York River. Reverend David Mossom, rector of nearby St. Peter's, performed the Church of England ceremony before a glittering assemblage of friends, relatives, officers of the army and navy, and colonial officials including Francis Fauquier, Lieutenant Governor of Virginia. The women in their silks and the men ablaze in scarlet coats embroidered in silver and gold gave warmth to the winter day as the great coaches arrived from neighboring plantations.

Washington, that tall soldier fresh from the wars, and the pretty widow deserved the admiring glances of the invited guests. The six-foot-two-inch Colonel was dressed in civilian blue. His coat was lined with crimson silk. He wore an embroidered white satin waistcoat, and there were gold buckles on his shoes and at his knee.

According to one report, "the bride was attired in a white satin quilted petticoat, and a heavy, corded white silk overskirt; high-heeled shoes of white satin, with diamond buckles; rich point-lace ruffles; pearl necklace, ear-rings, and bracelet; and pearl ornaments in her hair. She was attended by three bridesmaids."

The honeymoon, which lasted for nearly three months, was spent at Martha's house on the York River, and in Six-Chimney House in Williamsburg, the colonial capital. There, on Washington's 27th birthday anniversary, February 22, 1759, he took his seat for the first time in the Virginia House of Burgesses. There is an unverified tradition that Speaker Robinson welcomed him with such warmth that when the Colonel arose to acknowledge the tribute he was utterly speechless with embarrassment.

"He blushed, stammered, and trembled, for a second;

when the Speaker relieved him by a stroke of address. . . . 'Sit down, Mr. Washington,' said he, with a conciliating smile. 'Your modesty is equal to your valor, and that surpasses the power of any language that I possess.'"

Whether fact or fiction, this anecdote has the ring of authenticity. Throughout his life Washington was more effective in action than in oratory. Nevertheless he was to perform his new civic duties well. Obviously he satisfied his loyal constituents. Year after year they re-elected him to the House of Burgesses.

In a letter written at about this time, George Mercer, a fellow Burgess, described the Colonel as an imposing figure, "straight as an Indian, measuring 6 feet 2 inches in his stockings, and weighing 175 lbs . . . well developed muscles, indicating great strength. His bones and joints are large as are his hands and feet. He is wide shouldered . . . neat waisted . . . and has rather long legs and arms. His head is well shaped, though not large, but is gracefully poised on a superb neck. A large and straight rather than a prominent nose; blue-grey penetrating eyes which are widely separated and overhung by a heavy brow. His face is long rather than broad, with high round cheek bones, and terminates in a good firm chin. He has a clear tho rather colorless pale skin which burns with the sun. A pleasing and benevolent tho commanding countenance . . . In conversation he looks you full in the face, is deliberate, deferential and engaging . . . His movements and gestures are graceful . . . and he is a splendid horseman."

Quite possibly Martha considered him handsome and herself a lucky woman. He swiftly became the favorite of his two stepchildren, John Parke Custis ("Jackie") and Martha Parke Custis ("Patsy"), whose ages were respectively four and two. Washington, who could be a stern disciplinarian when training unruly troops, showed great tenderness toward these children.

A large order of goods which arrived from England in March of this year included a number of toys. For Jackie there was a little coach pulled by six horses, plus a tiny whip to make them gallop and a stable to house them. Among Patsy's presents were a neat walnut bureau and a small corner cupboard. One of the children was given a miniature watch and the other a child's fiddle. When Washington neatly penned long lists of goods to be purchased in England he never forgot the needs of his new son and daughter.

The master of Mount Vernon was eager to return to his beloved but "rundown" plantation on the Potomac, a place which Martha apparently had never seen. The big house had been closed and the buildings and fields badly neglected while Washington had been fighting on the frontier. Now he was anxious to put his estate in order and to plant spring crops.

It must have been something like a minor military maneuver to pack and move his family across the intervening miles of muddy roads and swollen creeks and rivers from the York to the Potomac River. But Washington, who had moved armies across mountains, could scarcely have been disturbed by the mere moving of a family!

However, he seems to have forgotten, until the cavalcade was on the road, how unprepared Mount Vernon would be for the arrival of his wife and the children. In a hasty note written on the first Thursday of April, 1759, he sent ahead instructions to his servant John Alton:

> Jon: I have sent Miles on to day, to let you know that I expect to be up to Morrow, and to get the Key from Colo. Fairfax's which I desire you will take care of. You must have the House very well cleand, and were you to

make Fires in the Rooms below it w'd Air them. You must get two of the best Bedsteads put up, one in the Hall Room and the other in the little dining Room that used to be, and have Beds made on them against we come. You must also get out the Chairs and Tables, and have them well rubd and Cleand; the Stair case ought also to be polished in order to make it look well.

"Enquire abt. in the Neighbourhood, and get some Egg's and Chickens, and prepare in the best manner you can for our coming . . ."

No chickens on that huge plantation? Presently Washington would find that he also needed to buy pork. Even the feed for animals must be purchased until a crop of hay and grain could be planted and harvested. And all of the buildings were in need of repair.

However, George Washington had never been happier than when on this flowering April he brought his little family to Mount Vernon. He could repair his buildings and his fortune, increase his herds and flocks, breed ever better horses and foxhounds, plant orchards of apples, peaches, cherries, pears and plums, vineyards of grapes, and groves of the "Mississippi nut" or pecan tree.

Although the soil of Mount Vernon was not of the best, Washington through sheer intelligence, good management and horticultural study would, in the years to come, support his family, his slaves and a little village of artisans on this estate. The flour from his mill at Dogues Run would become a well-established and highly saleable commodity.

Washington rightly believed that no estate in America "is more pleasantly situated." He called the Potomac "one of the finest rivers in the world; a river well stocked with various kinds of fish at all seasons of the year, and in the spring with shad, herrings, bass, carp, sturgeon &c., in great abundance. The borders of the estate are washed by more than ten miles of tide water; . . . the whole shore, in fact, is one entire fishery."

Fishing for sturgeon is a princely sport. Duck hunting was another of Washington's pastimes. Often he went foxhunting with his neighbors, dining afterwards at one or another estate.

After a day on horseback supervising the labor on his several adjoining farms, Washington enjoyed tea on the terrace overlooking the Potomac, a game of cards or billiards, and good conversation at his table which was seldom without guests (invited or otherwise). He loved to attend gay dances with Martha. In his ever busy mind he had endless plans for improving the buildings and fields of Mount Vernon, for draining great swamps or digging canals. All that he wanted of life was to live in this manner under his own "vine and fig tree" on his beautiful bluff above the "River of Swans."

In a letter dated about this time he summed up his contentment in a single sentence. "I am now, I believe, fixd at this Seat with an agreable Consort for Life and hope to find more happiness in retirement than I ever experience'd amidst a wide and bustling World."

CHAPTER 12

FIRST IN WAR,
FIRST IN PEACE

WASHINGTON HAD HOPED THAT HE COULD PUT AWAY his sword and live in peace for the rest of his life. For sixteen years that wish was granted. From the spring of 1759 to the spring of 1775 he enjoyed his family role as the master of Mount Vernon.

However, a great storm was brewing over the Atlantic. Trouble of a most threatening nature was arising between the British Government and the American colonies. King George III and some of his ministers looked upon the

New World as a source of revenue, to be exploited at the royal pleasure.

The once-loyal colonists were angered by a "long train of abuses." They resented the armed troops quartered upon them. They disliked the Stamp Act which taxed newspapers, pamphlets and legal documents. They were driven to violence by the tax on tea.

Some of these taxes were more of a nuisance than a crushing burden. But a principle was at stake. The colonists rightly insisted, "No taxation without representation."

More serious dangers lay in the severe trade restrictions imposed by the Mother Country which threatened the colonies with complete financial ruin. Worst of all were the frequent suspensions of the ancient legal rights and privileges "of freeborn Englishmen." Sometimes even trial by jury was denied to those who seemed unsympathetic to the Crown.

By 1769 George Washington had come to the conclusion that he and his fellow Americans must resist these "lordly masters." If refusing to buy British goods failed to bring the King to his senses, perhaps force of arms would be necessary.

As a member of the First and Second Continental Congresses, Washington was definitely opposed to further vain petitions to the British Crown. He still did not visualize separation from England, but he was unwilling to lose those "valuable rights and privileges . . . without which life, liberty and property were rendered totally insecure." From this point on Washington's life merges with the history of the American Revolution.

When the Minute Men at Lexington and Concord fired the shots "heard 'round the world" in April 1775, it became obvious that the thirteen colonies must quickly rally to oppose the arrogant British army. Three weeks after that first rattle of musketry, the Second Continental Congress met in Philadelphia to organize armed resistance and to choose a commander in chief. Washington protested his lack of military experience to fill the important office. He did what he honorably could to dissuade his friends from voting him to the supreme command. Nevertheless, after a brief debate, he was elected to the post—a decision of far-reaching consequence.

In writing to his wife Martha (whom he sometimes called "Patsy") he spoke with deep emotion of this new turn of events which would tear him away from family life at Mount Vernon:

> *My Dearest*: I am now set down to write to you on a subject which fills me with inexpressible concern, and this concern is greatly aggravated and increased, when I reflect upon the uneasiness I know it will give you. It has been determined in Congress, that the whole army raised for the defence of the American cause shall be put under my care, and that it is necessary for me to proceed immediately to Boston to take upon me the command of it.
>
> You may believe me, my dear Patsy, when I assure you, in the most solemn manner that, so far from seeking this appointment, I have used every endeavor in my power to avoid it, not only from my unwillingness to part with you and the family, but from a consciousness of its being a trust too great for my capacity. . . . But as it has been a kind of destiny that has thrown me upon this service, I shall hope that my undertaking it is designed to answer some good purpose . . .

Accompanying this moving and heartfelt letter was a new will he had drawn up providing for Martha and the family, should he be killed in battle.

Knowing as we do that under Washington's leadership America eventually won its great struggle for freedom, we are inclined to forget that the new commander in chief had real reasons for self-doubt. There was no question of his patriotism, his bravery or his will to win. But could this erstwhile frontier colonel, with scant battle experience and very little knowledge of strategy or the problems of high command, become overnight a great general able to face British commanders who had spent a lifetime learning their trade? "A kind of destiny" must have helped him in the ordeal that lay ahead.

Despite his modesty, from the very moment he took command at Cambridge, Massachusetts, in July, 1775, Washington demonstrated his ability as a leader. Ordering cannon to be brought overland from Fort Ticonderoga, he fortified Dorchester Heights overlooking Boston, forcing the far larger British Army under General Howe to evacuate the city on March 17, 1776. Such a victory caused even the not-too-easily-impressed New Englanders to hail Washington as a hero.

The successful siege of a city is one thing, but fighting a great war of maneuver is quite something else again. The odds were vastly against the great Virginian.

Among the terrible difficulties which Washington faced from the first were sectional prejudices among the colonists, the indifference or disloyalty of at least one-half of the American citizens, dishonest public officials, short-term enlistments among the soldiers, continual desertions, jealous and incompetent officers, and a chronic shortage of food, clothing, ammunition and money to pay the soldiers. The general staff of any army must write hundreds of orders and letters. Washington had few qualified aides to help him with this mountain of paper work.

Most baffling of all was the threat imposed by the enemy's great fleet which could move troops secretly and fairly swiftly from one point on the American coast to another. To outguess and outmaneuver the British Navy continued to be an almost impossible problem for Washington.

Nevertheless, with a few brave and loyal officers and a ragged but rugged little army, this fearless commander in chief continued to fight the Redcoats and the German mercenaries.

Washington and his army were driven from Long Island. They were driven from Manhattan. They lost forts Washington and Lee on either side of the Hudson River. Then came perhaps the darkest hours of the Revolution as Washington led his fast dissolving and deeply dejected troops in their weary and desperate retreat across New Jersey. At this point even Washington's resolution was briefly shaken. In a letter to one of his brothers dated December 18th, 1776, he wrote: "I think the game is pretty near up ..."

Yet such were this commander's recuperative powers, that only a week after this letter was written, he recrossed the Delaware in his surprise Christmas attack and overwhelmingly defeated the Hessians at Trenton. Then, slipping away like an "old fox," he achieved his great victory at Princeton before moving farther north to safe winter quarters.

During the next four years Washington himself fought but three major battles: Brandywine, Germantown, and Monmouth. Not one was a victory, although Monmouth might have been. His *real* victory was his ability to keep an army-in-being during such winters of suffering as that of 1777-78 at Valley Forge, and the even more terrible winter of 1779-80 at Morristown, New Jersey. No wonder some of the men mutinied in the camp near Morristown. Here again the snow was stained red with the blood of barefooted men. Ragged, cold, hungry and unpaid, these citizen soldiers somehow endured. But no commander could have struggled more valiantly with a reluctant Congress in his effort to feed and clothe his miserable army.

What builds morale? In addition to food, clothing, shelter and pay it is often the power of words. Washington had almost no talent in the use of language. It was Patrick Henry who said, "Give me liberty or give me death." It was Thomas Jefferson who wrote the noble phrases of the Declaration of Independence: "We hold these truths to be self-evident, that all men are created equal, that they are endowed by their Creator with certain unalienable Rights, that among these are Life, Liberty and the pursuit of Happiness." It was Thomas Paine who proclaimed, "These are the times that try men's souls . . ."

Great voices these, rising above the roar of the cannons, the groans of the wounded and dying and the curses of the hungry men.

But it was Washington who maintained an army in the field, keeping alive the ghostly hope of eventual victory. His final stroke of genius at Yorktown, in 1782, will be long remembered. Moving his troops swiftly to join the French, he took brilliant command of the allied forces in the final action which defeated Cornwallis. By the end of the war Washington had become a very able general.

During the next two years the commander in chief had a more subtle foe to fight. The war had been won, yet no peace had been signed. There was great restlessness among his unpaid soldiers and officers. Some wanted Washington to proclaim himself king. But Washington, for all his stern leadership in time of war, knew that America was destined to be a republic, ruled largely by the consent of the governed. He had no slightest desire to have himself crowned king. Washington found himself in a predicament as "critical and delicate as can well be conceived," being caught between "The sufferings of a complaining army on the one hand, and the inability of Congress and the tardiness of the States on the other . . ." Here were very real "forebodings of evil." It was quite possible in the late winter of 1783 that the unpaid army might have arisen, overthrown Congress and established a military dictatorship. All that was needed was a word from Washington, and he could have become a beneficent despot.

To curb this dangerous movement, Washington rose to one of his great moments. On March 15th, at a camp near

149

Newburgh-on-the-Hudson, he addressed the army, promising his services, to the utmost of his abilities, to right their grievances. But he went on to say:

> . . . let me entreat you gentlemen, on your part, not to take any measures which, viewed in the calm light of reason, will lessen the dignity and sully the glory you have hitherto maintained.

He begged the officers and men to rely upon "the purity of the intentions of Congress." Gradually he swayed his audience toward sanity, reducing the seething resentment of the rebels.

Then, in trying to read to the assembled men a letter from a member of Congress (concerning the complications which were delaying army pay), Washington stumbled over the words. Were his eyes growing dim after these many years of warfare and of paper work by candlelight? A hush descended as Washington reached into his pocket for his glasses.

"Gentlemen," said their beloved commander, "you must pardon me. I have grown gray in your service and now find myself growing blind."

If any in that audience had failed to be convinced by

Washington's logic, none failed to be moved by this simple admission that he had given his best in their service.

Washington's farewell to his officers at Fraunces Tavern in New York was another touching ceremony. But now his duty was done. He could relinquish his great commission and retire—permanently, he hoped—to Mount Vernon on the bluff above the Potomac.

Washington, however, was not to be allowed peace and tranquility. He needed time, now, to repair his plantation and his fortune. But he was given little leisure for either. So heavy was his correspondence that he sometimes felt himself a public clerk. Visitors descended on him like a plague of locusts. He spoke of Mount Vernon as a "well-resorted tavern." Soon he was deeply worried concerning the political health of the nation. Under the Articles of the Confederation, the states had become a bickering family of rival sovereignties, ready to splinter into thirteen jealous and quarreling little countries.

With some reluctance Washington became a delegate to the Constitutional Convention of 1787. His services in presiding over that great convention contributed largely to its eventual success in framing our strong and rational Constitution. It was principally because both Washington and Benjamin Franklin approved of the document that it was later ratified by the individual states.

Hoping again that this might be his final public service, Washington returned to Mount Vernon. Almost immediately it became apparent, however, that he could scarcely avoid being elected the first President of the United States. One cannot doubt that Washington was again quite sincere in his modest denials of capability. However, he was also a citizen who never shirked a duty to his country—unpleasant and demanding though it might be.

He was, of course, chosen our first President by the unanimous vote of the Electors. He was formally notified of his new honor. And he accepted the verdict with a dignified reply. Now he must prepare for the journey from Virginia to New York City, first federal capital of the United States.

If Washington thought himself unprepared for the Presidency, there was little evidence that anyone agreed with him as he rode northward through the beautiful April countryside. He was feasted and feted in Alexandria, Georgetown, Baltimore, Wilmington, Chester, Philadelphia, Trenton, Princeton, New Brunswick and Elizabeth Town. Many of these municipalities were associated with far grimmer occasions in his mind. Gentlemen escorts on horseback accompanied him from one town to the next. Salutes were fired from cannons. Speeches were made and toasts lifted in his honor. Bridges were garlanded with green leaves, and girls strewed flowers before him, singing songs composed for the occasion. Washington has been pictured as a stony-faced hero on horseback. But sometimes on this journey tears came to his eyes.

At Elizabeth Town Point a newly constructed and beautifully decorated barge was awaiting to take him by water to New York City. As he came up the harbor toward the Battery, flags of all nations broke out from the ships at mooring, cannon roared their welcome, and boatloads of singers came out to greet him.

There ahead of him lay the waiting throngs; the dignitaries; the ceremonies. Soon now he would be taking the awe-inspiring oath of office as the First President of the United States of America. Ahead too lay the great challenge and responsibility of making that office an honorable one. Washington had made his contribution in war. Now he would make his even greater contribution to the peacetime happiness, orderliness and prosperity of the nation he had done so much to create.

The voices came out to him over the water. The guns reverberated across the harbor. Every church bell on the island was ringing its welcome.

He would try, as he had always tried, to merit the trust and love of his countrymen, and to be worthy of those words yet-to-be-spoken—*First in War, First in Peace and First in the Hearts of His Countrymen.*

Index

ABOUT THE AUTHOR

STERLING NORTH is one of America's most beloved authors of books that appeal to all ages. Born in a small town in Wisconsin, he started his writing career at an early age. When he was eight years old one of his poems was published in a popular magazine for children. Throughout high school and college he continued writing stories, poems, and even song lyrics.

After he married and had two children, he went to work as a cub reporter for the *Chicago Daily News* where he soon became the newspaper's literary editor. Throughout his career he continued to write a book a year, including a number of bestsellers. His books have always been characterized by a warm and accessible style combined with careful research of the subject.

Mr. North won a Newbery Honor award in 1963 for perhaps his most famous book, *Rascal*, which has sold over a million copies. Several of his books, including *Rascal*, have been made into popular motion pictures.

BOOKS IN THIS SERIES

George Washington: Frontier Colonel
BY STERLING NORTH

John Paul Jones: The Pirate Patriot
BY ARMSTRONG SPERRY

The Stout-Hearted Seven:
Orphaned on the Oregon Trail
BY NETA LOHNES FRAZIER

Geronimo: Wolf of the Warpath
BY RALPH MOODY

Lawrence of Arabia
BY ALISTAIR MACLEAN

Admiral Richard Byrd: Alone in the Antarctic
BY PAUL RINK

General George Patton: Old Blood & Guts
BY ALDEN HATCH

The Sinking of the Bismarck:
The Deadly Hunt
BY WILLIAM SHIRER

★STERLING POINT BOOKS